A Suitable Design: How to Organize Your Writing

A Suitable Design

How to Organize Your Writing

John Harrington
Michael Wenzl

California Polytechnic State University

MACMILLAN PUBLISHING COMPANY
New York

Collier Macmillan Publishers
London

Macmillan Publishing Company
866 Third Avenue, New York, New York 10022

Collier Macmillan Canada, Inc.

Library of Congress Cataloging in Publication Data

Harrington, John, Date:
  A suitable design.

  1. English language—Rhetoric.   I. Wenzl, Michael.
II. Title.
PE1408.H345   1984   808'.042   83-11357
ISBN 0-02-350280-0

Printing: 1 2 3 4 5 6 7 8   Year: 4 5 6 7 8 9 0 1 2

ISBN   0-02-350280-0

Credits and Acknowledgments

Bill Bradley. *Life on the Run.* Copyright © 1976 by Bill Bradley. Reprinted by permission of TIMES BOOKS/The New York Times Book Co., Inc.

Eldridge Cleaver. *Soul on Ice.* New York: McGraw-Hill, 1968.

John McPhee. "Bill Bradley." From *A Sense of Where You Are.* New York: Farrar, Straus, Giroux, 1969.

Alfred North Whitehead. *The Aims of Education and Other Essays.* New York: Macmillan, 1929.

Richard Rhodes. *The Inland Ground: An Evocation of the American Middlewest.* New York: Atheneum, 1970.

Arthur F. Pillsbury. "The Salinity of Rivers." From *Scientific American,* Vol. 245, No. 1 (July 1981).

Payson D. Sheets. "Volcanoes and the Maya." From *Natural History,* Vol. 90, No. 8 (August 1981).

John E. McCosker. "Great White Shark." Reprinted by permission of SCIENCE 83 Magazine, copyright the American Association for the Advancement of Science.

Stanley Meisler. "Less Crime in Canada." From *The Los Angeles Times* (May 26, 1982).

Anita M. Collins, Thomas E. Rinderer, John R. Harbo, and Alan B. Bolten. "Colony Defense by Africanized and European Honey Bees." From *Science,* Vol. 218 (October 1, 1982). Copyright 1982 by the American Association for the Advancement of Science.

John Muir. "The Grandeur of Yosemite Falls." From *Yosemite.* New York: Appleton Century Crofts, 1912.

Herbert Kohl. "Physical Violence Aside, TV's Psychic Violence is the Real Cause for Alarm." From *The Los Angeles Times* (August 27, 1982).

PREFACE

We have written too many false starts for this preface. One- and two-paragraph beginnings litter our office. We have jumped up to smash empty soda cans, to straighten books, to reset the clock. After writing this book and several others, we still think that writing should not be so difficult. But it is. And we recognize the irony that in a book about writing we feel frustrated by needing to work so hard to explain to someone else how to write. Rubbing *A Suitable Design* like a magic lantern will not make you a good writer; this book has no magic genie. But we do present designs which will make the process of writing easier—not easy, just easier.

An understanding of the components of effective design will ease the task of writing. But it is important to recognize immediately that no single, pure design will serve for all the types of writing expected of people in school or in professions. Instead, most writing tasks require assembling the components of several designs. Description, for example, rarely appears alone. Writers seldom describe merely to describe. Rather, description usually contributes to a larger design, perhaps one explaining how one thing compares to another. A comparison of two backpacks, for example, might require describing the frame of each. The design for comparison might in turn contribute to an essay arguing in favor of buying one backpack instead of another. A writer would therefore use the design for description as a component contributing to a broader design for comparison, and the design for comparison would also be one of the major components contributing to the still larger design determined by the writer's ultimate purpose: arguing in favor of a particular backpack. In this text, we present the principles of effective organization and offer an inventory of designs in order to help students do two things: to recognize the elements of effective design and to be able to assemble their own suitable designs.

We divide this book into the three major sections found in every piece of writing: a *preparation* section which orients readers to what will follow; an *expansion* section which develops and clarifies the point of an introduction; and a *closure* section which brings a discourse to an end. Our *preparation* section concentrates on what writers can do to prepare themselves to write and on what writers can do to prepare their readers to understand what will follow. Our *expansion* section provides basic designs for fulfilling the promises a writer makes to a reader in an introduction. After explaining general strategies for developing a message, we present two different kinds of designs: *fixed designs* and *flexible designs*. The *fixed designs* are those which have, over time, developed structures for communications which recur regularly, such as inquiries, complaints, or research reports. The *flexible designs*, on the other hand, represent the traditional modes of discourse (description, narration, exposition, and argumentation) which provide components that can flexibly be formed and reformed to fit any situation a writer will face. Our *closure* section indicates the options a writer has for ending various kinds of discourses.

We discuss fixed designs before flexible designs for pedagogic reasons. While flexible designs obviously provide tacit strategies for fixed designs, our experiences suggest that at first students respond best to the guidance of prescriptive designs. By discussing first a few of the most common tasks a writer must do, we demonstrate to students that the designs for writing exist for a reason. They represent not the dictates of English teachers, but the collective wisdon of millions of writers who have found strategies for dealing with specific problems. In short, designs exist because they work.

But we designed this book so that a teacher need not start with— or even use—the fixed designs. We recognize that many teachers will choose to begin with one, two, or even all of the flexible designs and then return to their application in the fixed designs. Other teachers will ignore fixed designs in favor of the traditional modes taught in freshman composition. The design of this book will aid all such approaches. Obviously, this text can be read through from the beginning, but that isn't necessary. While the book's structure reflects the basic organization of a discourse, we assume that many readers will focus on particular segments according to need. We also hope that *A Suitable Design* will serve as a reference book in providing advice for coping with specific rhetorical situations. Summary boxes accompanying each design, for example, provide quick reference for a writer who recognizes that a particular rhetorical situation calls for a specific design.

We have also kept this book short. We want its readers to grasp the concepts quickly and to see immediately in the examples how other writers have applied those concepts. We have not provided materials for sustained analysis. Instead, we assume that this book will provide the rhetorical foundation for examining other writing, whether that writing be the product of seasoned authors or of fellow students. Hence, we present short readings to illustrate concepts concisely. While the principles we discuss need to be reinforced and extended, we want to keep this text as flexible as possible so that it will work with whatever other readings a class might address. Throughout, we have focused as sharply as possible on the components of effective design.

We take both our direction and our title from the first of the Elementary Principles of Composition in Strunk and White's *The Elements of Style* (New York: Macmillan, 1979). Strunk and White direct writers to "choose a suitable design and hold to it."

> **A basic structural design underlies every kind of writing. The writer will in part follow this design, in part deviate from it, according to his skill, his needs, and the unexpected events that accompany the act of composition. Writing, to be effective, must follow closely the thoughts of the writer, but not necessarily in the order in which those thoughts occur. This calls for a scheme of procedure. In some cases the best design is no design, as with a love letter, which is simply an outpouring, or with a casual essay, which is a ramble. But in most cases planning must be a deliberate prelude to writing. The first prin-**

ciple of composition, therefore, is to foresee or determine the shape of what is to come, and pursue that shape.

A sonnet is built on a fourteen-line frame, each line containing five feet. Hence, the sonneteer knows exactly where he is headed, although he may not know how to get there. Most forms of composition are less clearly defined, more flexible, but all have skeletons to which the writer will bring the flesh and the blood. The more clearly he perceives the shape, the better are his chances of success.

Whether in architecture or in writing, design can be reduced to three principles: all designs must exhibit a *purpose*, contain a *structure*, and provide *pleasure*.

All designs exist to do something. They have a function. Consequently, the *purpose* of design cannot be separated from its final form. All designers know they must anticipate how someone will use what they design. This is such a basic idea that most courses in design deal with it first. A design for a new library, for example, leads a designer to ask immediately how well a design will meet the needs of those who will use the library.

Questions of purpose dominate any consideration of a design for a physical object. A screwdriver looks the way it looks because of what it does. It could hardly be designed in another way and still perform efficiently its designated purpose. The *Declaration of Independence*—a creation clearly less physical than a screwdriver—also has a purpose, although it is more abstract than that of a screwdriver. While designs resting along a spectrum from most physical to most abstract all depend upon a purpose, they reveal that purpose most readily when a person can see their results—for example, a screw driven in or a new country formed.

Writing too has a spectrum. At one end might be the Sears catalogue and at the other a great novel. Most of what a person writes in business or school lies somewhere in the middle. To know the purpose of writing and to state it is the starting point for good writing. And the finishing point.

Structure achieves purpose. Structure's most important principles are efficiency and simplicity. A look through the history of all manmade designs reveals that most of the best have been simple and have done a job. But a good structure depends upon a clear purpose. Confusion about purpose, or attempting to achieve several purposes at once, thwarts both efficiency and simplicity. Consider the design of the Swiss Army Knife. Its many functions make it a considerable curiosity, but the more functions it adds the less efficiently it performs any one of them. A wad of extensions makes its cutting blade more difficult to use than a single-bladed knife. Its screwdriver helps with only rudimentary work. Its scissors or corkscrew replaces single tools only in moments of desperation. The Swiss Army Knife serves a useful function, though, as a cautionary image for writers. Any design should be as simple as possible to perform a useful function.

Although a designer begins with function, not esthetics, a good design provides *pleasure*. When function combines well with form, the result is almost always happy. Consider the classic lines of a carving knife compared to the protrusions of the Swiss Army Knife. Writers provide pleasure when a reader easily grasps their purpose and feels that the time put into reading has been well spent. The reader's reward lies in understanding, and understanding is pleasurable.

We hope that an understanding of the principles of design and an awareness of organizational components will help students to recognize and assemble their own suitable designs.

Several people have helped us or prodded us through this project. Jim Howland, George Kastner, Rolf Monteen, Al Landwehr, and Lynne Landwehr provided materials and advice. Diane Cummings and Linda Howe prepared the manuscript. At Macmillan, Tony English seeded and nurtured the project, Susan Didriksen provided timely editorial skills, and Joel Brauser carefully steered the manuscript through production. Our wives, Mary Kay and Linda, not only put up with us but often came to our rescue. To all, we offer what is never enough: thanks.

CONTENTS

PREFACE   vii

1. Preparation: 1
Readying Yourself and Your Reader

ORIENT YOURSELF   2
Consider the Roles You Play   2
Are You an Expert or a Novice?   3
Are You a Participant or an Observer?   4
Understand Your Choice of Roles   5
Locate Information   12
Know the Difference Between Facts and Judgments   14

DEFINE YOUR TOPIC   16
Find the Key Verb in a Writing Assignment   16
Limit Your Subject   18
State a Controlling Idea   20
Can You Make an Outline?   21
Are You Ready to Write?   22

WRITE YOUR INTRODUCTION   24
Orient Your Reader   24
Make a Good First Impression   29
Decide Which Kind of Opening to Use   31
Refine Your Controlling Idea As You Write   40

2. *Expansion: Developing the Message*   **43**

EXPANDING BY DESIGN   43
Expand by Addition   44
Select Your Additions   44
Order Your Selections   45
Allocate Space Within Your Order   46
Understand Paragraph Design   47
    Subject–Focus–Example Paragraphs   48
    Question-and-Answer Paragraphs   50
    Problem–Solution Paragraphs   51
    Transition Paragraphs   52
Choose Between Fixed and Flexible Designs   53

THE FIXED DESIGNS   55
Recognizing Fixed Designs   56
Requests   57
Complaints   61
Good News Messages   64
Bad News Messages   67
Research Reports   71

THE FLEXIBLE DESIGNS   80
Describing Objects   81
Narrating Events   88
    Typical Narrative Applications   89
    Process Designs   95
Explaining Concepts   106
    Comparison   108
    Classification   124
    Cause and Effect   130
Arguing Policies   139
    The Purpose of Argument   140
    Assumptions   141

Ethos   142
Foundations for Persuasion   143
Time Frames for Arguments   147
Fallacies   148
Reasoning Through Connections   152
Reasoning Through Examples   165

3. Closure: Finishing Up   179

REWRITING   179

KINDS OF CLOSURES   183
The Summary   183
The Appeal   184
The Question   185
Restatement of the Main Point   186
Just End   186

A Suitable Design: How to Organize Your Writing

1

Preparation: Readying Yourself and Your Reader

Consider ordinary tasks such as planting a garden or changing oil in a car. Would you plant before digging? Mix and scatter the seeds? Would you change oil with the car pointed down a steep hill? Unscrew the drain plug before placing the drip pan under the engine? You might think the methods obvious for planting gardens and changing oil, but watch a child (dare we include adults?) undertake a task for the first time. Only with experience do we see that for every task there is a plan that will make the chore easier and the results better.

As do other tasks, writing requires a plan. Personal writing (diaries, poems, certain letters) may tumble freely from your mind, but writing intended for less intimate readers takes careful planning. Besides, inspiration is fickle. How many minutes or hours will you wait for a voice to tell you what to say? Looking at the ceiling may conjure a pleasant memory, but it will not provide a plan and words. If it takes more time and energy to plant a garden or to change oil without a plan, logically it will also take more time and energy to write without one. Therefore, *all writing should follow a plan.*

Orient Yourself

All writing takes place at a certain *time*, in a certain *place*, for a certain *purpose*. Your history professor gives you one week to analyze the major economic factors contributing to the Revolutionary War. Your supervisor hands you a customer's letter requesting information about programs available for a computer that your company recently put on the market. The context is set. Your challenge is to spot key ingredients so that you can respond to the request.

Before setting to work, ask yourself:

1. *Who* is the reader and what will he or she expect?
2. *What* is the purpose of your communication?
3. *How* much do you know about the subject?

CONSIDER THE ROLES YOU PLAY

In describing last weekend, would you tell the same details to your mother, best friend, romantic partner, and math professor? Would you use the same wording for each person, or might your vocabulary be spicy in one instance and evasive in another? Would emphasis be the same, or might you stress certain events more to your best friend than to your mother? In both obvious and subtle ways, each person edits and selects with an eye to the way he or she wants the reader to react.

A writer also chooses words according to the knowledge and sophistication of the reader. Could we say "sophistication" if we wrote for children? Can you imagine discussing the principles of nuclear fission in identical ways with third-graders and a professor of physics? *Writing requires role playing.* Size up your role quickly. Understand your reader as well as possible under the circumstances; then you can begin to organize ideas so that your reader will understand them. When talking with someone, you probably select a role intuitively. With teachers, you play the student. With parents, you play the son or daughter. With a stranger, you might be aloof.

As a writer, though, you must often take on a role for people whom you have never met (e.g., a business contact in another city) or for people who can be only vaguely defined (e.g., the readers of a newspaper or of an essay in freshman composition). Even so, a key part of planning involves getting to know what you can about your readers to see the role choices imposed by your relationship to your readers. The differences between you and your reader in experience, attitude, and interest will govern the way you present yourself. To understand your readers better, ask yourself these questions:

1. What are your readers' backgrounds?
2. How much do they know? (Can the readers understand the material? Is it too simple?)
3. How will they use the information?
4. Will your message be welcome? Unwelcome?

ARE YOU AN EXPERT OR A NOVICE?

As a writer, you will usually find yourself in one of two roles: *expert* or *novice*. You don't choose, though. The expertise of your reader decides your role as a writer. A junior studying natural resources management is an expert when preparing a pamphlet for local junior high students on marine life in nearby tidal pools, but a novice when submitting a paper on the same subject to a professor with a Ph.D. in aquaculture. When you are a student, you write as a novice because the reader (a teacher) knows more about the subject than you do. But when the reader knows less—whatever your status—you plan the role of expert.

In both cases you convince your reader that what you say is accurate and valuable. As a novice, you earn a reader's respect by showing familiarity with the material, given your limited exposure to it. You may express some uncertainties, and your reader, who is more expert, will not be disappointed unless you show that you are unwilling to try or incapable of learning.

Experts have less luxury. Not only must an expert *sound convincing*, he or she must also *be accurate*. A reader will not accept an expert's errors lightly. When evaluating the paper on tidal pools, the professor of aquaculture would probably do little more than point out inaccuracies and assign a less than superior grade. But the junior high students reading the pamphlet would most likely lose confidence in—and perhaps sneer at—a writer whose mistakes they spot. An employer or client would probably do worse than sneer.

ARE YOU A PARTICIPANT OR AN OBSERVER?

Often students complain that they cannot write assignments they find dull. *Interesting*, in this case, means assignments that touch the writer's own experiences. Beginning writers prefer—and do best at —assignments that call for personal writing, especially assignments focused directly on themselves. People writing professionally, on the other hand, seldom consider whether an assignment excites them and rarely expect to write about strictly personal interests.

All writers, though, feel most comfortable when writing about something they know well. Beginners simply know little but their personal experiences, while those in professions have some sort of specialty that they know intimately. Based on a writer's relationship to his or her subject, we can set up a spectrum from the personal, firsthand experience of a *participant* to the more distanced and impersonal scrutiny of an *observer*.

A *participant* is involved and close to his or her subject. This closeness gives a participant access to detail usually denied the observer. The way an event "feels" is more important than any specific information. Because of high emotional involvement, a participant may have trouble recognizing the pattern or significance of a subject. Coolness and detachment do not characterize the participant's responses.

At the other end of the spectrum, a detached and aloof observer views matters in a way that he or she and others consider objective. An observer holds everything at arm's length to lessen emotional or prejudicial involvement. Focusing on the facts available, the observer searches for patterns and meanings that his or her mind can discern or invent.

Seldom, of course, does any writer rub against either end of the spectrum. But writers equally seldom manage to function simultaneously as observers and participants at the imaginary center of the spectrum. Often, time blurs memory and emotions, allowing one who was once a participant to become an observer. But this is a change from one point of view to another, not a combining of the two. Instead, most writers function in one role or the other.

Right or wrong, the *observer* has more status in our society. Our age accepts the notion that matters are best understood when studied and presented in a detached and objective way. While this may not always be valid, you need to recognize that people *believe* observers more readily than they believe participants.

As you gain experience, you will find fewer chances to write as a participant. The process of maturing takes each of us away from an emphasis on self. Who, after all, is more self-oriented than a baby? We begin immersed in everything, as Wordsworth says, and learn to move outside the self in a way that lets us see the world in terms other than those that affect us directly. Paradoxically, we must move away—gain distance—from certain things to understand and explain them to ourselves. How, for example, can we understand our upbringing until we have left our parents and see our upbringing juxtaposed with the way other people were raised?

UNDERSTAND YOUR CHOICE OF ROLES

Almost always, *novice* joins *participant* at one end of the spectrum and *expert* couples with *observer*. The more a writer tends toward observer-expert, the more the subject will dominate. The tone will be less personal. The writer fades into the background, putting the subject in the spotlight. The more one writes with authority, the more impersonal and formal the tone.

At the other end of the scale, novice-participants emphasize a dramatic presentation of the self. They focus loosely on a subject, but since facts, information, or explanatory theories are minimally available, they must ingratiate themselves with their audience. If the reader is not a close friend, the writer usually ingratiates by presenting himself or herself as personable, funny, or interesting. While a reader has little sense of "knowing" the expert-observer, the novice-participant beams a recognizable personality.

Context defines the writer's role. Experts automatically write as observers, generally using the third person (he, she, it, they), while novices rely primarily on the more personal first person (I, we). Good writers, though, sometimes break this mold because, as Walker Gibson deftly points out, the language of third person is "stuffy," while second person is "sweet" and first person is "tough." Good writers can liven up their prose by personalizing what they say or by speaking directly to their readers. But care is needed in breaking the mold that calls for distance for expert-observers and personalizing from novice-participants. The role of novice, for example, will seldom work when readers expect writers to be experts. The cuteness of "me" backfires. It will not supplant a firm, impartial presentation of information or analysis.

Here are some examples of writers presenting themselves as participants:

With Phil Jackson's substitution, the Knicks seem revitalized. He blocks two shots, steals three passes, and over a span of four minutes gets six rebounds. Walt Frazier hits four jumpers and we tie the score. Chicago seems befuddled. Jackson hits a hook across the middle and then takes a lead pass from Dave DeBusschere and dribbles the length of the floor for a reverse lay-up. Dick Barnett smiles and shakes his head, unable to comprehend how, despite his apparent awkwardness, Phil can get the job done. On the last series of plays in the first half, Jackson blocks his man from a rebound, only to see the ball bounce to a Chicago guard, who attempts a drive for a lay-up. Phil leaves his man, lunges across the lane as if out of control, and swats away the ball just as it is about to hit the backboard. Goal tending is not called. The buzzer sounds. The Knicks are up by three at the half.

I believe that basketball, when a certain level of unselfish team play is realized, can serve as a kind of metaphor for ultimate cooperation. It is a sport where success, as symbolized by the championship, requires that the dictates of community prevail over selfish personal impulses. An exceptional player is simply one point on a five-pointed star. Statistics—such as points, rebounds, or assists per game—can never explain the remarkable range of human interaction that takes place on a successful pro team. Personal conflicts between team members will never surface if there is a strong enough agreement on the community's values and goals. Members of the Budapest String Quartet disliked each other personally, but collectively still made exquisite music. They did so in part because they had a rigid score that limited the range of personal interpretation. The cooperation in basketball is remarkable because the flow of action always includes a role for creative spontaneity; the potential for variation is unlimited. Players improvise constantly. The unity they form is not achieved at the expense of individual imagination. That creative freedom highlights the game's beauty and its complexity, making the moment when the ideal is realized inspiring for the players, thrilling for the fans. . . .

—Bill Bradley, *Life on the Run*

1. What is the effect of the present tense narrative in the first paragraph?
2. What is the author's purpose? Does he state a controlling idea?
3. How does the viewpoint of a participant contribute to Bradley's purpose?
4. How would an observer approach the same topic?

My day begins officially at 7:00, when all inmates are required to get out of bed and stand before their cell doors to be counted by guards who walk along the tier saying, "1, 2, 3 . . . ." However, I never remain in bed until 7. I'm usually up by 5:30. The first thing I do is make up my bed. Then I pick up all my books, newspapers, etc., off the floor of my cell and spread them over my bed to clear the floor for calisthenics. In my cell, I have a little stool on which I lay a large plywood board, about 2½ by 3 feet, which I use as a typing and writing table. At night, I load this makeshift table down with books and papers, and when I read at night I spill things all over the floor. When I leave my cell, I set this board, loaded down, on my bed, so that if a guard comes into my cell to search it, he will not knock the board off the stool, as has happened before. Still in the nude, the way I sleep, I go through my routine: kneebends, butterflies, touching my toes, squats, windmills. I continue for about half an hour.

Sometimes, if I have something I want to write or type so that I can mail it that morning, I forgo my calisthenics. But this is unusual. (We are required, if we want our mail to go out on a certain day, to have it in the mailbox by about 8:00. When we leave our cells at 7:30 to go to breakfast, we pass right by the mailbox and drop in our mail on the way to mess hall.)

—Eldridge Cleaver, *Soul on Ice*

1. How does Cleaver's present tense narrative in the first paragraph differ from Bradley's?

2. What is Cleaver's purpose? Does he state a controlling idea?
3. How does the viewpoint of a participant contribute to his purpose?
4. How would an observer approach the same topic?

Here are some examples of writers presenting themselves as observers:

Bradley is one of the few basketball players who have ever been appreciatively cheered by a disinterested away-from-home crowd while warming up. This curious event occurred last March, just before Princeton eliminated the Virginia Military Institute, the year's Southern Conference champion, from the N.C.A.A. championships. The game was played in Philadelphia and was the last of a tripleheader. The people there were worn out, because most of them were emotionally committed to either Villanova or Temple—two local teams that had just been involved in enervating battles with Providence and Connecticut, respectively, scrambling for a chance at the rest of the country. A group of Princeton boys shooting basketballs miscellaneously in preparation for still another game hardly promised to be a high point of the evening, but Bradley, whose routine in the warmup time is a gradual crescendo of activity, is more interesting to watch before a game than most players are in play. In Philadelphia that night, what he did was, for him, anything but unusual. As he does before all games, he began by shooting set shots close to the basket, gradually moving back until he was shooting long sets from twenty feet out, and nearly all of them dropped into the net with an almost mechanical rhythm of accuracy. Then he began a series of expandingly difficult jump shots, and one jumper after another went cleanly through the basket with so few exceptions that the crowd began to murmur. Then he started to perform whirling reverse moves before another cadence of almost steadily accurate jump shots, and the murmur increased. Then he began to sweep hook shots into the air. He moved in a semicircle around the court. First with his right hand, then with his left, he tried seven of these long, graceful shots—the most difficult ones in the orthodoxy of basketball—and ambidextrously made them

all. The game had not even begun, but the presumably unim-
pressible Philadelphians were applauding like an audience at
an opera.

—John McPhee, *A Sense of Where You Are*

1. What is McPhee's attitude toward Bill Bradley?
2. How does Bradley's sense of basketball as a participant
   differ from McPhee's sense of basketball as an observer?
3. What does each consider most important?
4. Could McPhee's point be made as effectively by a
   participant?

The universities are schools of education, and schools of
research. But the primary reason for their existence is not to
be found either in the mere knowledge conveyed to the students or in the mere opportunities for research afforded to the
members of the faculty.

The justification for a university is that it preserves the connection between knowledge and the zest of life, by uniting the
young and the old in the imaginative consideration of learning.
The university imparts information, but it imparts it imagina-
tively. At least, this is the function which it should perform for
society. A university which fails in this respect has no reason
for existence. This atmosphere of excitement, arising from
imaginative consideration, transforms knowledge. A fact is no
longer a bare fact: it is invested with all its possibilities. It is no
longer a burden on the memory: it is energizing as the poet of
our dreams, and as the architect of our purposes.

Imagination is not to be divorced from the facts: it is a way
of illuminating the facts. It works by eliciting the general principles which apply to the facts, as they exist, and then by an
intellectual survey of alternative possibilities which are consistent with those principles. It enables men to construct an intellectual vision of a new world, and it preserves the zest of life
by the suggestion of satisfying purposes.

Youth is imaginative, and if the imagination be strengthened
by discipline this energy of imagination can in great measure
be preserved through life. The tragedy of the world is that
those who are imaginative have but slight experience, and
those who are experienced have feeble imaginations. Fools act

on imagination without knowledge; pedants act on knowledge without imagination. The task of a university is to weld together imagination and experience.

—Alfred North Whitehead, *The Aims of Education & Other Essays*

1. What does Whitehead say is the primary function of universities? In what ways would this point be more easy or more difficult to make if Whitehead adopted the stance of a participant?
2. Is Whitehead's language concrete or abstract? Is his use of language tied to his status as an observer? If you were to write this paragraph from the point of view of a participant, would you use the kind of language used by Whitehead?
3. Name the things Whitehead observes in order to make his point about universities. What is the effect of observing things other than universities?
4. What value judgments does he make? In what ways do his value judgments agree or disagree with your values?

The wheat in central Kansas in late June stands waist high. Each stalk is buff yellow, a hollow tube that no longer carries nutrients to the grain head, tapering to the diameter of a pencil lead at the top. Two, three, four joints along the length of the straw indicate the spurts of its growth through the long winter and short spring. At the top of the straw, bent over in the curve of a cobra's head, hangs the head of wheat, scaled and overlapped like a rattler's tail and loaded with about twenty-five grains of wheat, hardly enough to fill the palm of a cupped hand. But not like a rattler's tail either, for the grains in their husks advance up the head in a hardly noticeable spiral. From the cunning point of each husk of grain protrudes a fine tapering wire of straw; together these wires make up the wheat's beard—that is its name—and it is these wires of beard scraping together in the wind which give the wheatfield its characteristic sound, a whisper that is yet dry, a rustle, a high rattle as of some convention of small snakes, a miniaturization of cicadas, something insect-like, dry scraping of scaled legs. Our thirst for the oceanic must have led us to hear the ocean in a field of wheat, for that is not its true sound, but an insect concert, and part of the horror of the great locust plagues of the last century must have been the realization that the green horde outside the screens and windows and quickly stuffed chinks of the cabin sounded like nothing so much as a field of wheat come to terrible life. For if we eat the wheat, can it not also eat us? It is a fantasy any child might have, or any saint.

—Richard Rhodes, *The Inland Ground*

1. How does Rhodes' use of detail contribute to the purpose of the paragraph? What is the purpose?
2. Why does he use *our* and *we* near the end of the paragraph? Does the point of view of the paragraph change from *observer* to *participant* with the use of *our* and *we?*
3. Does the concluding speculation enhance or detract from the description of the wheat?
4. Locate at least three places in which Kansas wheat is implicitly compared with something else. What is the effect of the comparisons?

Here is an example of a writer presenting herself as an observer who was formerly a participant:

For sure, in a past that now seems to me as remote as prehistory, I too thought I would get married. I speak of my fifteenth, my eighteenth years of age. However, it's strange: the more my memory searches that time, the less I find the word "marriage." Even then it gave me a mysterious annoyance, like the words wife, husband, fiancée, betrothed. What I wanted as a girl, I suppose, was a man to love and by whom to be loved forever: as in the fairy tales. Yet I felt a threat in the fairy tale, a mortal risk: what if such a man kidnapped me for life? I have never been a domestic animal. I have never seen myself locked up in the small cosmos of the family. The profession of wife has always filled me with horror. I did not want to play the wife. I wanted to write, to travel, to know the world, to use the miracle of having been born. And, as if this weren't enough, I couldn't stand the idea of giving up my name to take the name of a man. To give it up, why? To annul myself like that, why? I was mine.

> Though confusedly, unawarely, I think I was at that time a feminist *ante litteram.* In fact, knowing I was a woman in a society invented and determined by men never gave me an inferiority complex, never put any limitations on my plans and on my dreams. On the contrary, it provoked and lit them. It was a kind of challenge.
>
> —Oriana Fallaci, *Why I Never Married*

1. What is Fallaci's purpose? Does she state a controlling idea?
2. Why does she shift tenses?
3. She selects the viewpoint of an observer who was a participant. How does this choice affect her purpose?
4. How would a writer approach the same topic from the viewpoint of participant only? an observer only?

LOCATE INFORMATION

You will find information from both internal and external sources. *Internal sources* are those already possessed by the writer: knowledge, ideas, methods. *External sources* include anything outside the brain of the writer: books, reports, computer tapes, another person's brain.

Don't confuse being "expert" with internal sources. Experts know what they need to find out and where to find it, but people cannot carry in their heads all the information about their specialties. Even the best experts need to double-check the information they file away mentally.

Writers determine what they need to know about a subject and then root it out. Writers who are experts will already know the sources for external information and will also (through experience) know how to tap internal sources. Less experienced writers need to find out how to locate information. Experts know, but novices need to be reminded, that good writing requires gathering more information than the writer needs. All good writing is a distilling process; more should go in than comes out. Having more information than needed makes the writer likely to recognize the right information. Writers *select* what is important. A writer with only one piece of information in his or her basket can only include that piece of information. The writer with a full basket can pick out the three best pieces.

To locate information from *internal* sources, ask yourself the following questions:

    I. What *is* the subject, or what does it *mean?*
       A. What are its primary *qualities?*
       B. What is its *function?*
       C. Can it be broken into *parts?*
       D. Can an *example* of it be given?
   II. What does it *resemble?* What is it *unlike?*
       A. Can it be put in a *group?*
       B. If not, what *excludes* it?
  III. What are its *origins, history,* or *causes?*
       A. Are there *multiple causes?*
       B. Can the subject be viewed as *cause? effect? means? end?*
       C. Does it *always* lead to a *particular effect?*
       D. What do you know about its *origins?* its *development?*
  IV. How do you know what you know about it?
       A. Firsthand experience?
       B. Reading? (How dependable are your sources?)
       C. Listening to others speak about it? (How dependable are they?)

To locate information from external sources, consider the following:

    I. Where is the information located?
       A. People: telephone or personal interview?
       B. Personal reference sources: notes, textbooks, reference works, previous research?
       C. Public reference sources: libraries, computers, governmental agencies, private agencies?
   II. Always state the unknown as a question. "Research" is another name for answering a question. When inquiring, ask general questions. Don't ask, "What information is available on Henry VIII's confiscation of church properties in the 1530s?" Ask "What information is available on Henry VIII's

dealings with the Catholic Church?" Otherwise, you may miss important background material.
III. Once you have asked general questions, ask more specific questions. (When did Henry confiscate church properties? What did he gain financially? What effect did his actions have on his political support?)
IV. After you investigate external sources, return to the list of questions for internal sources to discover any changes you might make.

KNOW THE DIFFERENCE BETWEEN FACTS AND JUDGMENTS

Is it a fact that the sun will rise tomorrow? That the temperature was 82 degrees Fahrenheit at noon in Los Angeles on July 22, 1981? That the Steelers are the best team in professional football? No, yes, and no. The sun probably will rise tomorrow since apparently it has done so for as long as anyone can remember. But it might not. Nothing in the future is ever certain. On the other hand, the temperature in Los Angeles may be verified. If you were not there or do not remember, you can check the records and talk with people who were there and do remember. In the third case, "best" is almost always judgmental—even if the Steelers happen to win the Superbowl.

Directly or indirectly, most writing assignments ask you to focus on facts, on judgments, or on some combination of both. For example, consider the following:

1. *Requests for facts:* A report for a geography class on the average annual rainfall in seven regions of the United States; an inquiry about the various kinds and prices of hardware that your company sells for wooden gates.
2. *Requests for judgments:* Which of seven areas in the United States has the best rainfall for growing alfalfa? which gate hardware is best for an inward-opening gate on Mr. Simon's redwood fence?
3. *Requests seeking both facts and judgments:* Evaluate the amount of rainfall in each of seven areas in the United States and determine which is most favorable for growing alfalfa; what are the differences among the three types of hardware your company

sells for wooden gates, and which type would you recommend for Mr. Simon's redwood gate?

In the first situation, the reader is not interested in your evaluation, only in the information you have available. A teacher may want to confirm that her students know certain kinds of information, and a customer may want to make an independent judgment about gate hardware based on the facts he or she gathers.

Some readers prefer judgments without detailed information, perhaps because the reader does not want to bother to master a complex subject. Usually those who seek only advice are in a rush or see a situation as relatively unimportant. With your toilet overflowing, would you go to various plumbing stores to seek information about possible solutions, or would you call a plumber for a quick remedy?

Most writing, though, requires both facts and judgments since few readers trust advice alone. If the writer is a novice, the reader wants to see whether the writer has grasped the facts of the situation and can make sense of those facts for some purpose. The expert combines information and judgment so that the reader can understand the writer's judgments and can examine closely (or have other experts do so) the evidence and logic supporting those judgments. Further, the expert wants to protect his or her judgments by showing how they were derived.

Does your reader seek mostly facts, mostly judgments, or judgments derived from explicit information?

The following is an example of a judgment combined with supporting facts:

> **More often, failure [in engineering] results from lack of imagination. The Quebec Bridge collapsed while under construction in 1907 because large steel members under compression behaved differently than the smaller members that had been tested time and again. The Tacoma Narrows Bridge failed in 1940 because the dynamic effect of wind load was not taken into account. Although designed to withstand a static wind load of fifty pounds per square foot, the bridge was destroyed by harmonic oscillations resulting from a wind pressure of a mere five pounds per square foot. We do not have to be too concerned about bridge failures anymore. (In 1869 American**

bridges were failing at the rate of 25 or more annually!) But the problem of reasoning from small to large, and from static to dynamic, is symbolic of the difficulties we face in designing anything in a complex, interdependent, technological society. The Aswan Dam is an example. As a structure it is a success. But in its effect on the ecology on the Nile Basin—most of which could have been predicted—it is a failure.

—Samuel C. Florman, *The Existential Pleasures of Engineering*

1. Identify Florman's judgment.
2. How do the facts help a reader to understand that judgment?
3. How does Florman refine his judgment after presenting his first two examples?
4. Can each example (Quebec Bridge, Tacoma Narrows Bridge, and Aswan Dam) be called a "fact"? In what ways is each example "factual"?
5. How does each example contribute to the judgment?
6. Given the facts Florman presents, could any other judgment be reached?

Define Your Topic

Once you understand your reader, determine the role your situation calls for, and gather information about your subject, it is time to define precisely what you want to say.

FIND THE KEY VERB IN A WRITING ASSIGNMENT

Point to your toe. *Hit* the fly. *Sit* quietly. Verbs tell a person what to do. As everyone learns in grade school, verbs spark the action of a sentence. Most assignments contain a verb pointing out what someone wants. Even in a vague assignment, an implicit command lurks in the background. An assignment may invite the writer to *analyze* a problem or to *interpret* some statistics. Many writers do poorly simply because they miss—or misunderstand—what the *key verb* tells them to do. The key verb works like a compass, telling the writer which way someone wants the subject directed.

Here are some key verbs that appear frequently:

DESCRIBE. This word asks the writer to use words to provide an image of something. To *describe* a Douglas fir is to detail its visible features.

ANALYZE. Coming from a Greek word meaning "to loosen," *analyze* always means to break down, or consider things, in *parts*. When *analyzing* pay attention to relationships. Consider the subject in parts to better understand the whole. To *analyze* the way a Douglas fir reproduces would be to break down the various stages of reproduction to consider what each stage contributes to the process of reproduction.

EVALUATE. To *evaluate* means to judge against some external standard. Although the writer considers both good and bad points, the evaluation normally leads to an overall positive or negative judgment. To *evaluate* the results of a sheer test on a Douglas fir board would be to measure the strength of the board against a scale established for such sheer tests.

INTERPRET. Often an assignment will ask you to determine or identify the *meaning* of something. What does it *mean* to say that a Douglas fir board loses 22 percent of its water when it is kiln-dried? The writer *interprets* the figure, indicating the significance of the 22 percent loss.

Here are some other "command words" writers often encounter:

Define	Summarize
Discuss	Compare
Explain	Prove
Demonstrate	Recommend
Relate	Investigate
Predict	

Every activity or discipline has its few key words. Know the words in your area. Usually the list is manageable, and you cannot afford not to know the words intimately. They tell you what your reader wants.

LIMIT YOUR SUBJECT

Rarely does anyone say "write anything you wish." Whether handed to you by employer or teacher, assignments come with limits. At first, most assignments seem a bit broad and vague: compare the economic condition of the South after the Civil War with that after the Spanish-American War; determine which crops will prove most profitable for lands owned by the Sunrise Corporation. The limits are seldom clear immediately. What ought to be included under "economic condition"? Is that "condition" the same throughout the South? What is the "South"? What does "after the Civil War" mean? And how will knowing the following kinds of information limit your study for the Sunrise Corporation? How large is the operation? What equipment is owned? How much capital is available to purchase new equipment if a certain crop requires such equipment?

Although these two assignments come with limits, the writer faces much work in limiting and defining the raw goods. The process is even more demanding with an assignment that is less clear (e.g., analyze the rise and fall of the Third Reich; compare *Hamlet* with *A Midsummer Night's Dream;* or—even more challenging—develop a paper from the contents of this course).

In an introduction, a writer stakes out the territory for which he or she will assume responsibility. This territory may be called the *scope* or the *limited topic.* Imagine looking out your window through a camera with a zoom lens. Beginning with a 30° area, you might see a mountain, sky with certain cloud formations, trees, houses, and so on. Imagine describing precisely all that you see through your viewfinder. Now zoom in to a 15° field. You can see half of what you saw before, but what you see is more detailed. The telescopic powers of your camera's lens might finally be so great that all you would see in the viewfinder would be a chimney, once distant. As a writer, you will often go through a similar process in limiting your initial topic. You move in and out with your zoom lens until you see what your reader needs to know. Everything that you see within the viewfinder is your responsibility as writer.

Some assignments, especially those given by teachers, force you to define a precise scope because an assignment is so vague that you could not handle the topic as is. Teachers often give vague assignments deliberately: students learn by sorting out what is important. For example, an assignment might ask you to investigate an early form of man. After learning about several forms of early man, you narrow your scope by concentrating on "Neanderthal man." But is clearly impossible to cover all of this topic in less than a five-volume series, so you look for subdivisions: Neanderthal man's geographical territory? use of shelter? body structure? cultural achievements? use of tools? social patterns? diet? The list gets long. You sort through the possibilities, choosing one. Perhaps you decide to write on the stone tools used by Neanderthal man during the late Pleistocene period in what is now West Germany. At this point, you see Neanderthal man in a context, and at the same time, you are ready to focus on a precise topic.

Narrowing a topic sounds easy, but isn't. The less you know about a topic, the foggier it seems. A significant part of the planning stage requires understanding a broad topic well enough to recognize its minor parts and how they all interrelate. Probably the easiest way to approach narrowing your scope is to ask the questions journalists have asked for years:

Who?
What?
Where?
When?
Why?
How?

These questions may not be enough, but they will get you started and will lead you to other questions growing more specifically from your topic. The trick in taking advantage of these questions is to be persistent in each category. One or two categories will probably prove more demanding than others. For example, *who, where, when,* and *how* will probably prove easy with Neanderthal man, but *what* and *why* ought to keep your brain busy for a while.

STATE A CONTROLLING IDEA

In a pocket billiards game, the cue ball sits still until hit by the cue. The cue ball then hits the other balls. The order is not random, but precisely determined by speed and angle. The skill of the player determines whether the speed and angle cause balls to slip into the pockets in proper order. The cue ball is like the writer's limited topic. It has no inherent direction. It goes nowhere without help. The action of the cue is like the writer's *controlling idea:* it propels the topic in a particular direction, causing the topic to touch (and direct) subtopics in a particular order.

The *controlling idea* makes an assertion—a point—about the limited topic. Alone, the topic has no inherent meaning. What is the significance of the stone tools used by Neanderthal man? An assertion about the topic provides a meaning that you can then explain. Once you see clearly the scope of your subject, you need to make an equally clear *point* about it. While "stone tools used by Neanderthal man" is a topic, note what happens when we give the topic a point: "Stone tools used by Neanderthal man *show little development* from the mid- to late-Pleistocene era." The topic now has *direction.*

Let's try another example. A writer concerned about agriculture in California decides to limit her topic to a particular crop, jojoba beans. After several more stages of limitation, she decides to assess the economic impact of the decontrol of oil prices on the jojoba bean industry in California. Her topic takes on a controlling idea when she adds a point, "The decontrol of oil prices *will aid* the jojoba bean industry of California *by increasing* demand *and causing* prices to rise sharply within six months of deregulation."

Pinpointing a controlling idea sounds easy, but it proves to be a writer's greatest challenge. Without the anchor of a controlling idea, a paper drifts. Ideas are delicate and elusive. Once you crystallize an idea and state it on paper, it sounds obvious. But often you will feel tongue-tied as you struggle to discover what you would like to say about your limited topic. We cannot give you a surefire way to identify controlling ideas, but we can tell you to think about the *point* you wish to make about your limited topic and we can pass on an old, but reliable, way to generate controlling ideas. (To understand the examples that follow, assume the scope of your assignment has been limited to "the pollution of inland waterways in New England during the past twenty-five years.")

1. *Define the key term(s) in your statement of scope:* "*Pollution* is industrialized civilization's poisoning of the natural environment." Purpose: to explain the consequences of such pollution.
2. *Compare (or contrast) the key term with something.* What is it like? unlike? "Pollution is worse in New England than it is in other areas of the country." Purpose: to compare the effect of pollution in New England with effects in other places.
3. *Account for the origin of the key term.* What brought about the present situation? What are its origins? How did matters get to their present condition? What are the causes? "Man's reckless disregard for his environment causes pollution." Purpose: to demonstrate how shortsightedness has created a major problem.
4. *What have the experts said about it?* What important testimony has been given about the topic? Positive or negative? Is the "expert" unbiased? Is the expert genuinely knowledgeable? "The most alarming of all man's assaults upon the environment is the contamination of air, earth, rivers, and sea with dangerous and even lethal materials" (Rachel Carson, *Silent Spring*). In this case, the expert's position can help you to establish your own either through agreement or through disagreement.

This method will get you started. Each of the examples could provide a controlling idea, but the purpose of the four questions is to lead your mind to consider your topic from several viewpoints. Usually you will find that one of the four questions will generate an idea that "feels" right. Then you need to find the words that will state the precise point you wish to make about your limited topic.

CAN YOU MAKE AN OUTLINE?

Some people outline elaborately and some write without one. Most writers at least jot down a few points before beginning. Frankly, we think some sort of outline, however simple, is essential unless the writer feels very familiar with the material. Rarely will anyone ask for your outline, but you will find that you will save much time by knowing where you will go next. You will probably modify your outline as you go, but that is the improvement generated by using the act of writing to think and to clarify.

Because outlining is, in practice, such an individual matter—varying greatly from writer to writer and from project to project by a single writer—we are reluctant to give strict marching orders about the subject. We can, however, pass on a bit of useful advice—advice that will apply equally to short papers and major treatises.

Outline by dividing your subject into three to six categories. You may use as few as two or as many as eight or more, but the middle range of numbers proves most useful. Two categories do little to divide the subject functionally and eight or more divisions are hard to control. A limited number of divisions also helps a writer to subordinate minor issues to major issues. Once you have laid out your three to six divisions for a five-hundred-word essay, you have the structure for the whole paper. For a larger subject, divide each section into three to six subsections. Very large subjects can be subsectioned as many degrees as necessary. (See "The Agony of Trying to Tell My Children" on p. 143 for an example of the sections of one essay.)

By the way, this system works well with standard note cards. You simply place the cards into three to six piles, subdividing the piles as appropriate until all your cards are in order and you are ready to write.

ARE YOU READY TO WRITE?

Let's review quickly what you need to do to prepare yourself to write.

   I. Define the content.
      A. Who is your reader?
      B. What is the purpose of the communication?
      C. What do you know about the subject?
  II. What stance will you take to communicate with your reader?
      A. Do you know your reader as an individual or as a member of a general category?
      B. What does he or she know?
      C. How will the information or ideas be used?
      D. Will the message be welcome or unwelcome?

     E. Are you an expert or a novice?

     F. Are you an observer or a participant?

III. Will your emphasis be on information, interpretation, or some combination of these?

IV. Have you established pertinent information by exploring *internal* sources?

     A. What *is* the subject and what does it *mean?*

     B. What does it resemble?

     C. What are its origins, history, or causes?

     D. How do you know what you know about it?

V. Have you located pertinent information by searching out *external* sources?

     A. Where is the information located?

     B. Ask general questions first.

     C. Next ask specific questions.

     D. Reconsider internal sources.

VI. Have you identified the key verb of the assignment so that you know what is expected of you?

VII. Have you sifted what you know to narrow your scope?

     A. Who?

     B. What?

     C. Where?

     D. When?

     E. Why?

     F. How?

VIII. Have you translated the limited topic into a controlling idea by making an assertion?

     A. By defining the key word of the limited topic?

     B. By comparing the key word with something?

     C. By accounting for its origin?

     D. By focusing on what the experts have said about it?

IX. Can you make an outline?

We began this chapter by saying that the process of writing should follow a plan. The foregoing questions provide a plan to help you prepare yourself to write. If you answer each question precisely and thoughtfully, you will have a fairly clear notion of the direction your writing ought to take. If you can invent a better plan, do so. If not, remember what happens to those who plant gardens or change oil without a plan. Unless you know a territory as an expert, a shortcut will probably not produce good writing. If you have answered these questions, you are prepared to write.

Write Your Introduction

Although learning to write is a "hands-on" experience, it takes a good deal of time to get ready to write. But the time pays off when you sit down to write your introduction with a clear sense of what you hope to accomplish.

ORIENT YOUR READER

A two-thousand-year tradition of beginnings can be summed up simply:

1. Give enough information to prepare your reader to understand your central idea.
2. Be brief.

"Be brief" sounds obvious but demands a firm sense of how much is enough. Often inexperienced writers divide short papers into three paragraphs: an introduction, a body, and a conclusion. This arrangement allows only one third of the paper for development, scarcely a balanced amount. Although every introduction is unique, most take up no more than 15 percent of the paper or report. An effective introduction tells a reader only what he or she needs to know to understand where your direction lies.

Introductions may have as many as four parts:

1. A controlling idea
2. Background
3. A list of subtopics
4. A hook

For emphasis, a *controlling idea* typically comes at an introduction's beginning or ending. For a one-paragraph introduction, the controlling idea will appear as the first or last sentence. In longer introductions, the controlling idea generally shows up in the first or last paragraph. No rigid rule says that controlling ideas need such placement, but it makes sense to put a controlling idea where it will stand out and be recognized by readers.

Some writers further emphasize controlling ideas by clearly prefacing them: "The purpose of this paper is to show . . ." or "I will demonstrate that . . . ." While formal writing, especially in scientific fields, relies on such obvious statement, most writers try not to resort to such stiff and formulaic statement. (See "State a Controlling Idea" on p. 20.)

Not all controlling ideas, though, should be placed at the beginning. Often the best design for persuasion or argument places the controlling idea at the end. Step by step, the writer leads the reader *to* the controlling idea. Sometimes, to be tactful, a writer states the controlling idea indirectly, implying rather than asserting it. When a writer wants to tell a reader something that the reader doesn't want to hear (e.g., that a loan application was denied), the writer deliberately buries the main point (bad news) in the text.

Examples of such situations can be found in the major organizational strategies in Chapter 2. Note, however, that such openings are rare. Expect to state a controlling idea clearly and unambiguously near the beginning.

Background includes whatever the reader needs to understand the controlling idea. The kind and amount of background will depend on your estimate of your reader. What will college freshmen in physics need to know to understand the principles of nuclear fission? How about readers of *Scientific American?* The more specialized a piece of writing, the more background will probably be needed, especially when the reader is not a specialist. Ask what your reader needs to know to grasp what you will say in the body. The following questions will start you thinking about what background to include:

1. *Do important terms need defining?* Your reader needs to know the precise meaning of any key words you use.
2. *What is important about the history of the subject?* Knowing about what has happened in the past may help a reader to understand the present situation.
3. *Is your own experience with the subject significant?* Your own

involvement may shed light on what you say in your controlling idea, especially if you write as a novice.

The following is a standard introduction setting forth background followed by the controlling idea.

Background {

Many ancient civilizations rose by diverting rivers and irrigating arid lands to grow crops. For such projects to succeed human beings had to learn to work cooperatively toward a common objective. The most fruitful of the ancient systems was created at the southeastern end of the Fertile Crescent, the broad valley formed by the Tigris and the Euphrates in what is now Iraq. From there civilizations spread eastward through present-day Iran, Afghanistan, Pakistan, India and thence into China, wherever rivers disgorged through valleys of recently deposited alluvial soil. At its peak of productivity each irrigated region probably supported well over a million people. All these civilizations ultimately collapsed, and for the same reason: the land became so salty that crops could no longer be grown on it. The salts that were washed out of the soil at higher elevations became concentrated in the irrigated fields as the water evaporated from the surface and transpired through the leaves of

Controlling idea {

the growing crops. Although floods, plagues and wars took their toll, in the end the civilizations based on irrigation faded away because of salination.

—Arthur F. Pillsbury, "The Salinity of Rivers"

1. Upon which of the four questions about background does Pillsbury focus (key terms, history, personal experience, or significance)?
2. Pillsbury presents his background as a narrative. How does his sequence of events lead to his controlling idea?
3. What is the value of referring to specific places, such as the Fertile Crescent?
4. Why does Pillsbury not mention salt earlier?

4. *Does the reader need to know why the subject, or your method of studying it, is significant?* Your particular approach or the subject itself may be unfamiliar to the reader, and you will need to make him or her see why your subject or your method is important.

Notice how often the word "significant" and "important" appear in these questions. Focus upon whatever is significant to your reader's understanding of your controlling idea.

A *list of subtopics* may be important to keep your reader oriented, especially in a long paper or report. A reader who knows what you

---

Here is an obvious presentation of subtopics:

> In this article, I summarize evidence of changes in achievement test scores from records of national testing and assessment programs and compare differential rates of change in mathematics and science with other fields.
>
> —Lyle V. Jones

Here is a more subtle use of a list of subtopics (see p. 143 for the full article):

> This is the time of the Jewish New Year, yet it feels more like Passover to me. My children are asking me four questions: Where, when, why, how?
>
> Earlier this week, my son Josh asked me where Lebanon was and when the killing began. His sisters wanted to know how it could ever have happened, and why Jewish soldiers had let it happen. They wanted to know what had become of us as a people.
>
> —Herbert Kohl

---

will discuss in each of your major sections will feel some sense of direction and be less likely to get lost. However, avoid such a list when your subtopics are based on time or other methods of organization that your reader will easily recognize.

A *hook* is a gimmick designed to catch a reader's attention. You see one kind of hook when you stand at a supermarket checkstand and gaze at the sensational blurbs on the fronts of pulp magazines inviting you to test your marital compatibility or promising to tell you the inside information on a famous singer's divorce. Seldom, though, will you need a hook unless you write for a popular magazine. When a hook appears, it comes first. In the kinds of introductions you are likely to write in school or business, a hook will typically run only a sentence or two, although some writers build whole introductions around hooks. (See the next section.) Generally, hooks offer striking facts, intriguing questions, interesting anecdotes, quotations from famous people, or moralistic sayings. Here are a few examples of short hooks.

Here an *anecdote* is used as a hook:

Along the shore, they were starting to feed the bodies of the dolphins into mechanical shredders. It's difficult to describe the revulsion. There were hundreds of bodies, and hundreds of dolphins still alive, but trapped in the tiny bay, leaping, churning the waters in anguish, as they watched and heard their companions die. By late in the afternoon of the first day, the sea seemed a boiling red, dyed by the blood of the dolphins, and the shore was grossly strewn with mutilated corpses of dolphins, waiting their turn to be ground by the shredders.

—Form letter from Greenpeace

Here *statistics* are used as a hook:

By the time a person is fourteen, he will witness 18,000 murders on the screen. He will also see 350,000 commercials. By the time he is eighteen, he will stockpile nearly 17,000 hours of viewing experience and will watch at least 20 movies for

every book he reads. Eventually the viewing experience will absorb ten years of his life.
                                        —John Harrington, *The Rhetoric of Film*

Most writers use a hook to gain the attention of a reader only when that is unlikely to happen on its own. Most writing you do will not require a hook. The cuteness or manipulative cleverness of hooks can annoy readers of routine reports, articles, or correspondence. You may sound a bit too much like a hustler or a wise acre if you always insist on trying to hook your reader. Use sound judgment.

MAKE A GOOD FIRST IMPRESSION

Your reader's needs determine the way in which you shape any introduction. Informed readers require only brief orientation, whereas those unfamiliar with a subject need more preparation. A report prepared for your supervisor, a person quite familiar with your project, may need little background information; a report on the same subject prepared for a client will probably demand a good deal of background.

Not only must you estimate your reader's familiarity with your subject, you must also "speak the same language." Effective communication happens between people who share something: a belief, a set of experiences, a specialty, a goal. Your inventory of what you share with your reader will probably begin with language, since it is the basic element most people share. All professionals—engineers, accountants, truck drivers—share a way of talking about work. This challenges you in two ways: to write so that someone from either your own or another profession will understand and to avoid the jargon of your own field unless your reader knows that jargon.

Be conscious of the assumptions your reader will make about you by the way you write an introduction. Your success in establishing contact with your reader will depend largely upon your ability to make a good first impression, not only with your content but with your tone and wording.

How would you react to the following introductions?

We aren't about to give you credit in our store because your terrible credit record reveals an irresponsible consumer. (Will you go there now for your cash purchases?)

The newtron bomb in my opinion, is a good deterent to keep other people from trying to conqor our country and take it over and inslave us to they're own eval purposes. (Do the spelling and grammar suggest someone whose analysis can be trusted?)

You can also go wrong by not showing firm control over content. Stating the obvious in your introduction might make your reader think you see him or her as a simpleton. How would you respond to such self-evident assertions as these if they appeared as the first sentences in essays?

One's first year at college involves a lot of adjustments.

Nuclear weapons are a threat to humankind.

Love is important to everyone.

You can also go to the other extreme by not telling something important, leaving your reader to see you as insensitive or oblivious:

The situation in the Accounting Department needs attention. (What situation?)

The actions of the central character in the novel were not believable. (What novel? What character?)

Another good way to lose a reader's confidence in you is to hint that you are not quite competent to write on the subject or, worse yet, to say something like "Although I have little knowledge of the situation, I feel I can offer excellent advice on how to remedy it because of my vast knowledge and experience as a human being."

In each of these cases, what you say and how you say it only work to create a poor first impression. You will find it tough to get a reader back on your side.

DECIDE WHICH KIND OF OPENING TO USE

For simplicity, we have divided openings into four categories:

Current status
Forecast
Hook
Personal contact

Your understanding of your reader's needs will govern your choice.

Current status openings focus on background information that will help a reader to grasp the writer's point. You will probably use this opening more than any other. It is the standard opening for most reports and papers. While experts usually concentrate on the current status of the *subject* (a summary of what is known or of what a reader needs to know), novices typically emphasize the effect that the subject has had upon them, explaining the status of their *understanding* of or *attitude* toward the subject.

Here are a few examples of *current status* openings:

Using familiar events to begin orienting the reader

> The hazards of living in a volcanically active area were dramatically illustrated by the May 18, 1980, eruption of Mount St. Helens in Washington. The lateral blast killed dozens of people and destroyed 150 square miles of forest, while the ashfall disrupted agriculture and transportation hundreds of miles downwind. Less obvious than the disadvantages of living in a volcanic area are the advantages, which include the fertile soils that develop as volcanic ash weathers. In fact, the agricultural productivity of the state of Washington owes much to the periodic eruption of the Cascade volcanoes during the past 10,000 years. My recent archeological research in El Salvador has

Orientation to the writer's focused topic

> revealed a similar balance of risks and benefits for the southeastern Maya people, who lived along the volcanic axis of Central America. About A.D. 260, a massive explosion buried these highlands in ash, forcing the Maya to abandon them for decades—up to two centuries in the worst hit areas. One small area in this region was struck by three additional eruptions in the years that followed. These various eruptions differed in terms of the size of the area devastated and the nature of the

Controlling idea

tephra (ash and other materials) blasted into the air, but in each instance people showed a dogged determination to reoccupy the lands affected, thereby reaping the benefits of volcanic activity. El Salvador's volcanoes not only influenced the course of Maya civilization but also preserved, for archeologists, a very detailed record of prehistoric times.

—Payson D. Sheets, "Volcanoes and the Maya"

1. What kinds of information about background does Sheets provide (key terms, history, personal experience, or significance)? Point to where he uses each, and explain why he does so.
2. How do these elements of background prepare for his controlling idea?
3. Why does Sheets begin by talking about volcanoes rather than about the Maya civilization? Why doesn't he begin with an orientation to his focused topic?

Controversial subject, introduced by Brewster's perception of what the *objections* to tenure are.

Of all the folkways of university life, perhaps "tenure" is least comprehensible to those whose professional or executive life involves the staffing of other forms of organized activity—business, finance, government, or non-profit service. In prosperous times the tradition of academic tenure evokes puzzlement. In times when colleges and universities are struggling for financial survival, tenure is challenged with increasing frequency.

How, it is asked, can we talk glibly about the knowledge explosion or the exponential rate of change—with all its risks of rapid intellectual obsolescence—and at the same time lock ourselves into lifetime obligations to people in their mid-thirties? Not only do we risk becoming stuck with the obsolete, but we remove the most popularly understood incentive to higher levels of performance. Furthermore, since even in financially easy times university resources are finite, every "slot" mortgaged for a full professor's lifetime blocks the hope for advancement by some promising members of oncoming generations. When resources are so tight that the faculty must be pruned, because of tenure most of the pruning is at the expense of the junior faculty. Many juniors are more up to date in their command of new methods and problems in fast-moving

fields, and many of them are more talented than are some of
the elders.
        —Kingman Brewster, Jr., "Should Colleges Retain Tenure"

1. What kinds of information about background does Brewster provide (key terms, history, personal experience, or
   significance)?
2. Do you think he supports or opposes tenure?
3. Later in the article, Brewster indicates that he firmly supports tenure. Why doesn't he state his support firmly in a
   central idea at the beginning?
4. Now that you know his stance, why do you suppose he
   points out various objections to tenure?
5. Before Brewster points out objections to tenure, he says in
   the first paragraph that tenure is difficult for many people
   outside the university to understand. Why doesn't he simply begin with the objections to tenure?

Background
focusing
on Swift's
present
understand-
ing of the
subject

It is a melancholly Object to those, who walk through this great
Town, or travel in the Country; when they see the *Streets,* the
Roads, and *Cabbins-doors* crowded with *Beggars* of the
Female Sex, followed by three, four, or six Children, *all in Rags,*
and importuning every Passenger for an Alms. These *Mothers,*
instead of being able to work for their honest Livelyhood, are
forced to employ all their Time in stroling to beg Sustenance
for their *helpless Infants;* who, as they grow up, either turn
Thieves for want of Work; or leave their *dear Native Country,*
to fight for the Pretender in Spain; or sell themselves to the
Barbadoes.
        I think it is agreed by all Parties, that this prodigious Number
of Children in the Arms, or on the Backs, or at the *Heels* of their
Mothers, and frequently of their *Fathers,* is *in the present*
deplorable State of the Kingdom, a very great additional Griev-
ance; and therefore, whoever could find out a fair, cheap, and
easy Method of making these Children sound and useful Members of the Commonwealth; would deserve so well of the Pub-
lick, as to have his Statue set up for a Preserver of the Nation.
        —Jonathan Swift, *A Modest Proposal*

1. What kinds of information about background does Swift provide (key terms, history, personal experience, or significance)?
2. What problem does Swift seem to point to in his opening two paragraphs?
3. What relationship does he try to establish with his reader? What assumptions does he make about his reader?
4. *A Modest Proposal* is a satire. Eventually, Swift proposes that Irish children be raised, sold, and butchered for profit. Through his outrageous proposition, Swift uses satire to focus on the plight of the Irish. In what way does his introduction help to prepare for his real purpose?

Forecast openings announce what the writer intends to do with the topic and explains what will follow. The writer assumes that the reader needs no more background than the simple forecast will provide. Such openings usually occur when a writer knows that the reader is almost as well informed on the issue as the writer, making immediate background unnecessary. All important information follows in the body. Here are several examples of *forecast* openings.

The following is a forecast opening, stating a list of subtopics and the controlling idea in a single sentence:

List of
subtopics
{
Dramatically declining job opportunities in academe, rapidly rising costs, and reduced financial aid for graduate students are combining to threaten both the quality of graduate education in the arts and sciences in this country and ultimately the continuity of scholarship in basic fields of knowledge.
    —William G. Gowen, from *The Chronicle of Higher Education*

The following is a forecast opening with a brief background:

Controlling
idea
{
This TourBook has only one purpose: to make your trip as enjoyable as possible by providing accurate, detailed information about attractions and accommodations in the area through which you are traveling. No attraction, hotel, motel, resort or restaurant pays for a listing. Each is listed on the basis

Back-
ground

> of merit alone, after careful inspection and approval by a AAA Field Representative. Annual revision of all the material in the TourBooks ensures that you receive the latest information available at press time.

List of
subtopics

> The What To See section of the TourBook describes many scenic, historic, recreational and other attractions which can add immensely to the scope of your trip. The Where To Stay— Where To Dine section, introduced by the vertical black strip, contains detailed listings for the best of lodging accommodations and dining establishments in the region. Comprehensive introductory pages explain the listings, tell how accommodations and restaurants are selected and outline how the rate guarantee applies to hotels, motels and resorts.
> In addition, you will find a number of maps—some keyed to accommodations listings by zone—of major cities, national parks and other areas of particular importance in the area covered by this volume. Also provided are a temperature table, a chart of driving distances and a list of AAA clubs through whose territories your trip will take you. Population figures are based on the latest reports of the U.S. Census Bureau.
>
> —Automobile Association of America, *AAA Tourbook*

The following is a forecast opening that limits the subject by telling the reader what the writer plans to do:

> For three thousand years, poets have been enchanted and moved and perplexed by the power of their own imagination. In a short and summary essay I can hope at most to lift one small corner of that mystery; and yet it is a critical corner. I shall ask, What goes on in the mind when we imagine? You will hear from me that one answer to this question is fairly specific: which is to say, that we can describe the working of the imagination. And when we describe it as I shall do, it becomes plain that imagination is a specifically *human* gift. To imagine is the characteristic act, not of the poet's mind, or the painter's, or the scientist's, but of the mind of man.
>
> —Jacob Bronowski, "The Reach of Imagination"

The following is a forecast opening that implies a list of subtopics too long to include.

> Writing an "F" paper is admittedly not an easy task, but one can learn to do it by grasp of the principles to use. The thirteen below, if practiced at all diligently, should lead any student to that fortune in his writing.
>
> —Joseph C. Pattison, "How to Write an 'F' Paper"

1. How do *forecast* openings seem to differ from the other openings?
2. In each of the *forecast* openings given, what kinds of information about background does the writer provide (key terms, history, personal experience, or significance)?
3. Which of the four examples most makes you want to read on? Which least makes you want to read on? Why?
4. Explain the assumptions that each writer seems to make about his readers.

Some introductions use a hook before a current status or a forecast opening, but others rely so much on the hook that catching the reader becomes the goal. In such cases, the hook combines with a statement of purpose to form the introduction. You will see this strategy used primarily in popular publications. (Look at any issue of *Time* or *Newsweek*.) The writer lures the reader with something enticingly related to the subject. Usually such introductions rely on interesting statistics, quotations, stories, anecdotes, or even definitions. Let us look at several kinds of hooks.

Here are two examples of hooks that use statistics to begin opposing editorials written for a college newspaper:

> The figures are appalling. In tanks alone, the U.S.S.R. now outnumbers the United States by over four to one, at 48,000 to 11,560. Soviet troop strength is well over twice that of ours, at 4.84 million to 2.09 million.
>
> The U.S. artillery force of 5,140 is dwarfed by the U.S.S.R.'s 19,300, and our submarines are outnumbered by 249 Soviet subs.
>
> —Tom Kinsolving, *Summer Mustang*

So Ronnie and the Pentagon brass are planning to increase America's already bloated war budget by an unprecedented $1.5 trillion over the next six fiscal years. That is the price tag, our leaders tell us, to keep the Commies from walking down Main Street, U.S.A.

—Mike Carroll, *Summer Mustang*

Here is an example of a hook that uses a quotation:

Quotation
> *For all these accumulated associations with whatever is sweet and honorable, and sublime, there yet lurks an elusive something or the innermost idea of this hue which strikes more of panic to the soul than that redness which affrights in blood. This elusive quality it is which causes the thought of whiteness when divorced from more kindly associations and coupled with any object terrible in itself to heighten that terror to the furthest bounds.*
>
> —Herman Melville, *Moby Dick*

Allusion
Herman Melville could feel it. Peter Benchley made box office history with it. And now it has captured me. It is the embodiment of something at once terrifying and enchanting, repulsive and inviting. It is the great white shark, a vision of sheer beauty and power, an animal that has earned the unforgiving hate and fear of all seagoing peoples of all time. Yet despite its fame, the great white shark has always remained a creature more of art than science. However, some recent eye-to-eye encounters with more than a dozen white sharks off southern Australia and a four-day experience with a 300-pound female in San Francisco's Steinhart Aquarium have led me to some intriguing ideas about what makes this great fish do what it does. Those stories, and what is to follow, are not unlike Mr. Benchley's fish tale—entertaining, at times unbelievable, but for the most part still an understatement.

Background

Controlling idea

—John E. McCosker, "Great White Shark"

Here is an example of a hook that uses an anecdote:

Anecdote

> In a Canadian Western published in 1910, a Royal Canadian Mounted Police officer walks into a gambling den and orders a desperado to lay down his gun. No blazing gun battle follows, as surely would in an American Western. Instead, the desperado meekly lays down his gun and silently slinks from the room.

Extending quotation

> "Irresistible authority seemed to go with the word that sent him [the Mountie] forth," novelist Ralph Connor wrote, "and rightly so, for behind that word lay the full weight of Great Britain's mighty empire."

Background

> Canada has a far lower crime rate than the United States, and some criminologists believe that part of the reason lies in the mythology reflected in that scene with the authoritarian Mountie and the slinking desperado. Other experts, while acknowledging the tradition of law and order in Canada, attribute the low crime rate in Canada to more modern factors—a lack of racial ghettos and racial frustration in the cities, strict control of handguns, and the small number of drug addicts.

Controlling idea

> Whatever the reasons, there is no doubt about the low crime rate. No matter how crime statistics are lined up and examined, they reveal astonishing differences between the United States and Canada.

> —Stanley Meisler, "Less Crime in Canada"

1. In each example, what does the hook contribute to the writer's introduction?
2. In each opening, what kinds of information about background does the writer provide (key terms, history, personal experience, or significance)?
3. Explain the differences between Kinsolving and Carroll in the way they use statistics.
4. What do McCosker and Meisler gain by including quotations and allusions, as well as background?
5. Explain the assumptions each writer seems to make about his readers.

You are probably more familiar with the final kind of opening, *personal contact*, than with any other. When you write a letter, you generally establish personal contact before developing your point. While an impersonal or objective stance characterizes reports or formal papers, letters obligate a writer to personalize. Letters open and close with a ritualistic handshake of personal contact: "Dear Soandso" and "Sincerely yours." The traditional colon following the salutation ("Dear Mr. Soandso:") adds some formality to most business correspondence, but personal contact remains. Instead of writing for a series of readers unknown to the writer, as in many reports and papers, the letter writer addresses a particular person who is capable of responding at a personal level. A magazine writer never expects to hear from those reading his or her articles but a letter writer usually expects some sort of response. The first paragraph— or more—of the letter establishes that personal contact. A letter from a business acquaintance of ours, for example, uses a current event plus a personal reference to establish contact:

> **By the time you receive this, Sky Lab will have fallen to the earth somewhere, and the tension will be over. The matter is in doubt at the moment, however, and I must say I admire your pluck in choosing a residence with *that* number [1313] on Palm Drive.**

Some letters don't rely on personal contact because they are not really letters at all. The familiar "letter to the editor," for example, is actually on editorial written by a nonprofessional for a particular newspaper's readers. Similarly, some who write for a broad readership manage to establish personal contact with readers, usually by adopting the style of letters. And we all receive those form letters that use computers to give the illusion of personal contact:

Dear Sam Cedarwood,

You and your family may soon have a shiny new Buick Skylark sitting in your driveway at 10021 Brightwood Drive.

A friendly computer has filled in a blank for your name and your address.

REFINE YOUR CONTROLLING IDEA AS YOU WRITE

Even a good controlling idea can get better. When you begin writing, a mental process starts—one that would not have started otherwise. Perceptions, connections, and bright ideas pop into mind. Writing leads to the unanticipated. Don't plod along clinging to your first controlling idea regardless of new notions. The human mind refines ideas in the most unexpected places and times. If you allow yourself to be "locked in" once your identify a controlling idea, you may find yourself pushing the proverbial square object into a round hole as you force your finished product to fit your first intentions. Writing is a way of knowing. Let your central idea grow more precise—or even change—as you discover meaning by stating it.

A controlling idea is much like the hypothesis relied upon so heavily by scientists. No scientist simply "studies" something, just as no writer writes on "just anything." Instead, a scientist states an hypothesis that is then subject to verification or proof. As with the *assertion* used by a writer to pinpoint a controlling idea, the hypothesis is the scientist's cue. The scientist and the writer simply strike different sets of billiard balls. Both find it important not simply to let things happen as they may, but to direct and test ideas by systematically exposing them to evidence, reasoning, and theory. If the ideas hold up, fine. But there is nothing wrong with changing hypotheses or controlling ideas, often significantly, in light of what testing reveals.

A useful rule: *Any controlling idea can be improved in the process of writing.*

EXERCISES

1. Select a recent political event and write four separate introductions to a discussion about that event: current status, forecast, hook, and personal contact. Since purpose and audience will govern which opening you will use, name the purpose and audience to which you will direct each introduction.
2. Rewrite one of the examples of each of the four kinds of introductions by turning each into another kind of introduction. For example, find a way to change a current sta-

tus opening into a hook or a personal contact opening into a forecast.

3. In three separate paragraphs, describe three roles you play.

4. In three separate paragraphs, describe three roles played by someone you know well, such as a relative or close friend.

5. Select a subject you know something about. Be sure that the subject is focused enough so that you can say something worthwhile about it in a single paragraph (for example, not baseball, but bunting in Little League; not alcohol, but problems with alcohol at rock concerts). Write one paragraph about the subject as an expert and one paragraph as a novice.

6. Select an event in which you were once a participant but that happened long enough ago that you can view it as an observer. In one paragraph, describe the event as a participant, and in another describe it as an observer. If possible, describe it in a third paragraph as an observer who was a participant.

7. Select something at which you are an expert or something at which you are a novice. Invent a specific situation in which you tell a reader (a) how you achieved your expertise, or (b) the steps you will take to become an expert.

2

Expansion: Developing the Message

Once you discover systematic approaches to prepare yourself and your reader, select a suitable design to expand the purpose identified in your preparation section.

Expanding by Design

By the time you trace the steps outlined in Section 1, you will begin shaping in your mind (if not on paper) what will follow. Sometimes the design for the whole discourse will come to you in an "aha!" moment of clarity during the preparation phase. If so, jot down the design immediately. Don't chance forgetting what might be an important insight. More likely, though, you will need to work a bit to find a suitable design. And even a good idea for a design will need testing. The suggestions that follow will give you both a method for developing a design and questions to help test the suitability of your first ideas for a design.

43

EXPAND BY ADDITION

All writing grows by addition. Does this sound obvious? Probably so, but sometimes the obvious needs pointing out. Even at the level of the sentence, expansion comes by addition. Children move from rudimentary verbal expressions (the command "Ice cream!"), to complete sentences ("May I have some ice cream?"), and on to sentences showing qualification, subordination, and detail ("If I do the dishes and clean my room, may I have a dish of strawberry ice cream for dessert, Dad?"). All versions contain the same request (ice cream), but by *addition*, the communication has taken on more complex dimensions, both of courtesy and of information.

At every other level, writing also expands by addition. Paragraphs contain clusters of sentences because the writer adds more complex information or qualification about the key idea of the paragraph. Sections contain paragraphs, and the whole discourse contains sections for the same reasons. The process of addition can be logical and sensible, or it can be whimsical and confusing. An irony about nonfiction prose is that most people claim to value brevity, but often behave as if more is better. It isn't. After a certain point, addition has little value. But a writer must counterbalance brevity against completeness, seeking the point where addition leads to understanding.

SELECT YOUR ADDITIONS

If you follow the steps in Section 1, you will have more information than you need. You cannot use everything that you learn from outside sources and that you discover while pondering the subject. Two things guide you in selecting what will expand your controlling idea: *audience* and *purpose*. (Audience and purpose will govern all other aspects of selection as well, including point of view, level of language, and kind of detail.) Always ask what will make your reader understand your purpose.

No formula can tell you how to select what is appropriate in particular situations, unless the situations are so repetitive that they can be reduced to a fill-in-the-blank form. Selection finally requires sensitivity and judgment. Be cautious about trusting your memory for what you will need. Memory is rarely systematic. Recall and selection differ greatly. Recall does not discriminate: it simply evokes memories from the depths of the mind. Selection requires a more rigorous process of consideration guided by purpose and a sense of how what is said will affect the reader. Recall your most embarrassing moment with a member of the opposite sex. Which details would you select for the following: an essay on this subject for an English class, a letter to your best friend telling about the incident, a "Dear Abby" letter (written under a pseudonym) asking advice about the incident? Notice how purpose and audience affect the details you select in each case.

ORDER YOUR SELECTIONS

Suppose that you have four pieces of film for a movie you are making: a close-up of a girl with a sad face, a close-up of a girl with a smiling face, a shot showing a girl looking in a bakery window, and a shot of a smiling baker walking to the window and picking up a pie. Now let's order these shots in two different ways:

girl looking in window	girl looking in window
sad face	happy face
baker picks up pie	baker picks up pie
happy face	sad face

The content remains unchanged; only the happy and sad faces were transposed. But a movie audience will perceive the scenes quite differently. In the first, the audience probably will assume that a kindly baker gave a pie to a hungry girl; in the second, the audience will assume the hopeful girl will go away without any pie. The baker's smile will probably seem unkind or evil. Although only two parts of the order changed, the audience takes away different meanings. The order of presentation contributes significantly to what a person understands.

The same process occurs in writing. What a writer says first assumes primary importance. Each succeeding piece of information qualifies and affects whatever follows. Reread the foregoing paragraph, for example. How would you respond if the paragraph began by explaining the meanings of the two shots, listed the shots, asked you to try to order some shots, described the shots, and then explained that the shots belonged to a hypothetical film? Each added sentence conditions the way in which a reader understands and reacts to what follows.

Two kinds of order dominate our lives: chronological and physical. We perceive time as linear: "This happened, and then that happened" or "She said, and then I said." The ability to tell or write simple narratives develops early in children, and either listening to stories or recounting events occupies much of the time of adults. The ability to describe physically develops similarly in us. We ask "What does it look like?" A child describes a monster drawn by her friend: "It was large and red and had yellow eyes and a forked tail."

We all share the ability to communicate through chronological and physical patterns. When all else fails, we return to these proven orders. If a person cannot explain what someting *means*, it is still possible to tell what happened or to describe what it looked like. Matter and time furnish the simplest orders for communication; others require logic and the ability to see patterns that the mind develops. We give detailed attention to all these orders later. For now, remember that when you become confused about design, you can always return to narration (telling events) or description (picturing in words), both of which focus on concrete things you can see or hear or touch.

ALLOCATE SPACE WITHIN YOUR ORDER

How much needs saying about each of the areas you select to include? *Selection* and the *allocation of space* touch each other closely, but they differ. *Selection* is a question of quality; *allocation* is a question of quantity. A writer asks *how much* detail, *how much* evidence, or *how many* reasons must be presented to accomplish the goal. The decision to allocate space is a decision about what to *emphasize*.

It takes careful judgment to allocate space to each of the sections you plan to include, and such judgment hangs on how clearly you understand your reader, your purpose, and your subject, all of which get defined during the first stage of preparation. Whichever order you select, your perception of the rhetorical situation, rather than some objective scale, will govern your allocation of space. Even seemingly objective scales of time or space are not *experienced* objectively. If you have ever been in a situation that threatened your life, for example, a car accident or a fire, you know that your normal sense of time changes. Dramatic events often seem to take much longer to occur than our usual sense of clock speed would suggest. That is one of the reasons filmmakers use slow motion for moments of intense experience.

Writers do not treat all details equally but, instead, assign space based on significance. A *résumé*, for example, recounts certain kinds of details of a person's life, usually for an employer. A person writing a résumé chooses the specific details that seem appropriate to a job being sought rather than interesting but inappropriate details of the writer's life, such as favorite television programs or deodorants. In short, a writer does not describe, narrate, or explain the world "as it is," but selects information, orders that information, and allocates space to that information based on his or her understanding of the rhetorical situation.

UNDERSTAND PARAGRAPH DESIGN

Most people know what a sentence is and how to put one together. Sentences can be organized in a limited number of patterns, with slots set aside for certain kinds of words. (Put a few of the words in the last sentence into different slots—for example the preposition "with" after the noun "slots"—and see what happens.) Beyond the level of the sentence, structure seems vague. This occurs mainly because the larger levels or writing allow much more room for choice.

Many people say that they paragraph intuitively or whenever they think the page will look better with an indentation. It is hard to fault such notions because so few writers consider analytically where to paragraph. Most writers just do it. Yet some people write better paragraphs than others, and noticing paragraph organization might help to develop a sense of paragraph development.

Some of the best advice about paragraphs comes from H. W. Fowler (author of the standard reference book *Modern English Usage*) who says that the purpose of paragraphing is to rest the reader, saying, in effect, "Have you got that? If so, I'll go on to the next point." Rules can't be laid down for the length of a paragraph, but Fowler counsels moderation. Too many short paragraphs irritate, and long paragraphs intimidate. The point is that paragraphs form units of thought rather than units of length. When you finish developing a thought, end the paragraph.

Paragraphs grow by addition. A point (usually found in a topic sentence) holds together the various statements and pieces of information. The point also generates whatever follows: qualifications, details, examples. Each bit added to a paragraph modifies what has gone before, sharpening the point of the paragraph. A look at a few paragraphing designs might help to prepare you for some of the challenges of paragraphing.

Subject-Focus-Example Paragraphs

You have probably heard many times about this standard paragraph. The writer announces a subject, narrows the focus of the announced subject, and provides details and examples to amplify the paragraph's point. Here is a typical example of a subject–focus–example paragraph:

> Not that the handicapped should be kept out of sight: far from it. They should be seen much more than they are—in buildings they can't enter right now because of swinging doors, or climb in because of escalators, or even get to because of transport design—so that people can get used to them. "We can't make the town over for gimps," a waggish friend once said to me, and this may go for Grant's tomb, St. Peter's dome and the Coney Island fun house. But new buildings are something else. Instead of telling the handicapped, it just happens—and if you don't adjust, it's your tough luck—simply let them in the door and up the stairs. That's all they ask. And if this isn't precisely a right—there aren't really all that many rights—it's at least a reasonable tax for the healthy to pay on their luck.
>
> —Wilfrid Sheed, "On Being Handicapped"

Sheed announces his subject—the appearance of the handicapped in public—and then narrows it to the notion that they should be seen more than they are. Sheed next provides examples of how problems of access prevent the handicapped from appearing in public and then pinpoints the kind of attitudes that perpetuate problems of access. Sheed further narrows his focus to new buildings and what can be done to recognize reasonable rights of access for the handicapped. But not every example of this paragraphing design is so neat.

Consider the following example:

> In our society (that is, advanced western society) we have lost even the pretence of a common culture. Persons educated with the greatest intensity we know can no longer communicate with each other on the plane of their major intellectual concern. This is serious for our creative, intellectual and, above all, our normal life. It is leading us to interpret the past wrongly, to misjudge the present, and to deny our hopes of the future. It is making it difficult or impossible for us to take good action.
>
> I gave the most pointed example of this lack of communication in the shape of two groups of people, representing what I have christened "the two cultures." One of these contained the scientists, whose weight, achievement and influence did not need stressing. The other contained the literary intellectuals. I did not mean that literary intellectuals act as the main decision-makers of the western world. I meant that literary intellectuals represent, vocalise, and to some extent shape and predict the mood of the non-scientific culture: they do not make the decisions, but their words seep into the minds of those who do. Between these two groups—the scientists and the literary intellectuals—there is little communication and, instead of fellow-feeling, something like hostility.
>
> —C. P. Snow, *The Two Cultures*

Snow begins with a strong assertion—his announced subject—that "we have lost even the pretense of a common culture." He narrows his focus and indicates the direction he will take by saying that people with the most advanced educations cannot communicate with each other. He then briefly describes—at a high level of generality—some of the implications of this state of affairs. Not until the second paragraph does he provide examples by explaining the gap in communication he finds between scientists and literary intellectuals.

Snow takes two paragraphs to announce his subject, narrow his focus, and provide examples. By isolating an example—about scientists and literary intellectuals—Snow focuses particular attention on these two groups. He could have presented the same sentences in a single paragraph, but he sharpens his point in this case by separating a logical unit into two sections. Because most paragraphs use some variation of the subject–focus–example design, keep the pattern in mind when you write.

Question-and-Answer Paragraphs

Do you suppose the design for a question-and-answer paragraph is more complex than the design for subject–focus–example paragraph? Actually, the two designs are not much different. The writer begins by posing a question and then answers it. The question announces the subject; then the writer focuses the topic and provides clarifying examples. For example,

> Was the partner's effect a consequence of his dissent, or was it related to his accuracy? We now introduced into the experimental group a person who was instructed to dissent from the majority but also to disagree with the subject. In some experiments the majority was always to choose the worst of the comparison lines and the instructed dissenter to pick the line that was closer to the length of the standard one; in others the majority was consistently intermediate and the dissenter most in error. In this manner we were able to study the relative influence of "compromising" and "extremist" dissenters.
> —Solomon E. Asch

> Now what do we see in the twentieth century, and increasingly in the last ten or twenty years? If I could put it as an introductory remark in the same way as I formulated my last remark about the nineteenth century, I would say that now everybody is a thing and nobody resents it. I could also put it this way: we have overcome the vices of the nineteenth century and are very proud of it—as the French were proud of the Maginot Line built according to the strategic thinking of the First World War. But we do not know that in overcoming the vices of the nineteenth century we have developed new vices which may be worse, or at least as bad. Because we are looking backward, because we are lazy, we tend to be smug; we are very satisfied

in looking back and therefore are blind to the moral problem of today.

—Erich Fromm

Problem-Solution Paragraphs

Few issues are so simple that they can be stated as a problem and given a solution in a single paragraph. But such paragraphs do pop up, and the strategy can be highly effective. Sometimes the writer will state the problem as a question, leading some to think that the problem–solution paragraph and the question–answer paragraph are one and the same. They aren't.

The following examples will demonstrate the difference:

If you have never done any whittling or wood carving before, the first skill to learn is how to sharpen your knife. You may be surprised to learn that even a brand-new knife needs sharpening. Knives are never sold honed (finely sharpened), although some gouges and chisels are. It is essential to learn the firm stroke on the stone that will keep your blades sharp. The sharpening stone must be fixed in place on the table, so that it will not move around. You can do this by placing a piece of rubber inner tube or a thin piece of foam rubber under it. Or you can tack four strips of wood, if you have a rough worktable, to frame the stone and hold it in place. Put a generous puddle of oil on the stone—this will soon disappear into the surface of a new stone, and you will need to keep adding more oil. Press the knife blade flat against the stone in the puddle of oil, using your index finger. Whichever way the cutting edge of the knife faces is the side of the blade that should get a little more pressure. Move the blade around three or four times in a narrow oval about the size of your fingernail, going *counterclockwise* when the sharp edge is facing right. Now turn the blade over in the same spot on the stone, press hard, and move it around the small oval *clockwise,* with more pressure on the cutting edge that faces left. Repeat the ovals, flipping the knife blade over six or seven times, and applying lighter pressure to the blade the last two times. Wipe the blade clean with a piece of rag or tissue and rub it flat on the piece of leather strop at least twice on each side. Stroke *away* from the cutting edge to remove the little burr of metal that may be left on the blade.

—Florence H. Pettit, *How to Make Whirligigs and Whimmy Diddles*

After posing a problem and talking about misconceptions that people might have about it, the paragraph focuses on a solution. The writer could have started with a question, but it might have seemed awkward and artificial. It certainly would have affected the *tone* of the paragraph. Too heavy a reliance on the question–answer format for paragraphs can grate on a reader.

Often problem–solution paragraphs make effective conclusions, especially for difficult material. In such cases, the problem–solution design allows the writer to summarize the primary issues that have gone before. Here is the last paragraph of an essay called "Creationism Isn't Science":

> **So the creationists distort. An attack on some parts of Darwin's views is equated with a rejection of evolution. They conveniently ignore that Darwin merely proposed one of many sets of ideas on *how* evolution works. The only real defense against such tactics lies in a true appreciation of the scientific enterprise—the trial-and-error comparison of ideas and how they seem to fit the material universe. If the public were more aware that scientists are expected to disagree, that what a scientist writes today is not the last word, but a progress report on some very intensive thinking and investigation, creationists would be far less successful in injecting an authoritarian system of belief into curricula supposedly devoted to free, open rational inquiry into the nature of natural things.**
> **—Niles Eldredge, "Creationism Isn't Science"**

In his essay, Eldredge identifies places that creationists go wrong in their thinking. The final paragraph shows that the problem (the creationist suspicion, mistrust, and misunderstanding of the scientific approach) could be solved by an educated understanding of how science really operates. Or, to put it another way, knowledge will alter views held in ignorance.

Transition Paragraphs

Although paragraphs can be any length, the shortest usually help lead the reader from one part of a discourse to another. Transition paragraphs can be as short as a single word and may run only a sin-

AN EXERCISE IN ADDITION

> *The object of this exercise is to send a letter to a friend (of your sex) from high school who now attends a college two hundred miles away, inviting him or her to a party.* Select *the pieces of information you would include, place them in an effective* order,and *indicate how much space you would allocate to each. To allocate space and to establish order, place pieces of information in categories that would become* paragraphs *and indicate the purpose for each paragraph. Add ten more details of your own.*

1. The friends giving the party live in an apartment.
2. The friends' apartment has laundry service.
3. The party starts at 7 P.M.
4. Party giver 1 loves cats.
5. Party giver 3 hates smoking.
6. Their apartment is usually a mess, but they have hired someone to clean for the party.
7. Party giver 3 rarely studies.
8. Party giver 1 always wears jeans.
9. Three people are giving the party.
10. Party giver 2 smokes a pipe.
11. The rug will be rolled up for dancing.
12. Party giver 3 always wears a tie.
13. Party giver 2 has a steady girlfriend.
14. The apartment is two blocks from your dormitory room.
15. The party will be given on Saturday, April 25.
16. Party giver 1 rarely washes his hair.
17. Party giver 2 has blond hair.
18. Party giver 3 drives a red Porsche.
19. An old friend you both know from high school said he would bring his band for an hour or two.
20. Party giver 2 works nights but has Saturday off for the party.
21. Everyone needs to bring something to drink.
22. Party giver 3 has a rich father.
23. Party giver 1 usually goes to bed at 10 P.M.
24. Party giver 3 is active in student government.
25. The apartment has a telephone.

26. *Your roommate will be gone for the weekend, and your friend can stay with you.*
27. *Party giver 1 smokes.*
28. *All the party givers are male.*
29. *You haven't seen your friend for two months.*
30. *Your grades went down last term.*

---

gle sentence. They provide a bridge to the next section of the discourse, functioning like a large punctuation mark that says, "I've finished with this part, and I'm now going someplace new." For example, after summarizing the case for abolition of capital punishment (saying that it is discriminatory, "unusual," and cruel) in the first part of an essay, William F. Buckley, Jr. makes a transition of the second half of his argument in a simple, one-sentence paragraph:

> **Viewed the other way, the question is whether capital punishment can be regarded as useful, and the question of deterrence arises.**

The paragraph clearly announces a change in direction (we will now view something from another angle) and then indicates the new direction the essay will take (from arguments against capital punishment to a consideration of whether it might usefully deter potential murderers).

Most paragraphs rely on the subject–focus–example design, but too much of the same thing can lull readers. Vary the length of your paragraphs, and be sure they do not get too complex for your reader to follow.

CHOOSE BETWEEN FIXED AND FLEXIBLE DESIGNS

If you write a proposal for a company, you will probably use a *fixed design;* if you write about property tax increases in a letter to the editor, you will probably choose a *flexible design*. Fixed designs structure your writing explicitly from beginning to end, and the writer expects to follow the accepted form. These designs have been developed for specific readers in a specific contex (usually professional or academic), and any deviation from the form will be noticed unfavorably. Flexible designs, however, provide general strategies for arranging a discourse. The reader doesn't expect information in any particular order, at least as long as the writer makes sense.

You probably can think of situations where you have used each kind of design: a fixed design for a lab report in biology (perhaps a design asking only that you fill in the blanks) and a flexible design for an analysis of a short story in a literature class. Fixed designs tend to be easier to apply because some problems of design do not occur. It is also easier to reproduce (or imitate) the fixed designs than it is to work out designs of your own. Consequently, we will look first at *fixed* designs and then move on from the sense of structure they provide to *flexible* designs.

The Fixed Designs

The first time you write about any subject—microbiology, history, sports—you will probably feel confused about how to shape what you know. But once you have actually written several reports for a microbiology course, you will know the parts of a good report, the order in which they ought to go, and the approximate length of each. Some kinds of writing recur so often that you need only find or recognize patterns familiar to those who do similar writing regularly. If you are lucky, someone will guide you to a design. As a student, you might find a professor of biology furnishing you with samples of well-written lab reports. As a new employee, you might find your supervisor at General Electric handing you a writing manual so that you need only look up "Progress Reports" to find the company's design. When not given help directly, you can usually find a design by looking for it in good samples. If you are writing a lab report in chemistry for the first time, read a few good reports, paying close attention to their *selection, order,* and *space.*

Imitating good designs is one of the best things a writer can do.

The practice of imitating writing of proven value increases the skills of the imitator, just as imitating improves skills in swimming or tennis. Also, finding a design can keep you from suffering "writer's block"—those terrifying periods when you know you have to write but can do no more than stare at a blank page. Picking out a pattern—a prefabricated design—and filling it out can itself be the mother of invention.

Surprisingly, you can decide on a design before you know the details of what you will say. After all, that is what many professionals do. A person who regularly writes environmental impact reports knows the shape of each report before getting down to particulars. So do those who write news stories. So do those who write engineering proposals. Knowing a design ahead of time simply makes writing easier. Since fixed designs tend to show up most often in business and school, you can probably discover a fixed design for most of what you write. We will point out a few designs that, over time, have become standardized so that you may see how and why they work and so that you may try them out.

RECOGNIZING FIXED DESIGNS

If you write a case study for a business administration class, a feasibility study to determine whether your company will buy a new computer, or a sales report for your supervisor, you will probably use a *fixed design*. Such designs are "fixed" in two ways: explicitly (rules set by professor, boss, government regulation) or implicitly (custom set by those who do such writing). Sometimes, for example, a company will *explicitly* tell you how to write a progress report. You will be told what belongs in each section of the report, what headings to use for each section, the order of the sections, and the approximate length of the report. At the same time, an *implicit* order exists for progress reports. By custom, progress reports include certain kinds of information in approximately the same order. If you write a progress report for another company, you will probably not find the precise formula assigned by the first company, but you will certainly recognize the same elements.

Fixed designs offer certain advantages. Some of the difficult decisions you face as a writer have been made for you. Not only do fixed designs furnish prefabricated categories for your information and ideas, but the rhetorical situation will also be defined. Most fixed designs focus on the needs of readers whom you know personally (especially teachers and readers of business letters) or who share a common level of either education or expertise. Further, readers of fixed designs already know and understand the pattern you present and why you chose it. A store manager, for example, reports weekly in the company's president in ways both have become accustomed to over time, or a student gets to know what a professor looks for in a lab report for organic chemistry. Readers of fixed designs have specific expectations about what they read. Because such readers look for certain things in a certain order, a writer knows what will please the reader.

The following sections present a sampling of the common fixed designs, along with a brief outline of a typical structure for each. These designs represent proven ways of handling each kind of writing, although you might see these same designs in other places with slightly different orders or approaches. None of these designs represents the only way to go about writing on the subject, but each suggests a *good* way to do so. If a design does not fit your purpose, alter and adapt it. But be careful when you make changes. These are *implicitly fixed designs* (unless a teacher plays the role of employer and says using a certain design is "company policy"), and consequently they set forth the collective wisdom of many writers over many years. These designs represent an easy way to understand the principle and importance of effective design. By trying out a few of these designs, you will see the advantages of good design and the need for a suitable design when you write for less precisely defined situations.

REQUESTS

Requests ask your reader to do something for you, usually something so routine that you do not need to worry about convincing your reader to do it. Typically such letters request *information* (for example, from a camera repair company about the cost of repairing a lens you dropped, from a canoe maker for a brochure, or from an aircraft manufacturer about details on the wing design of a particular plane for a research project.) In other requests, you might *order something* (550 balloons with your company's logo or an unusual birthday present for your mother) or *invite someone to do something* (a state senator, asking her to speak at your school's graduation ceremony).

A Design for Requests

1. *Preparation.* The first paragraph should state clearly *what* you want, *why* you want it (briefly), and *who* wants it, if that needs explanation. (You might be writing on behalf of someone or a group, or you might wish to identify yourself if that might affect your reader's response.)

2. *Expansion.* Explain your request. Make one point, and only one point, in each paragraph. Usually, your most important points will come first, but you may choose to lead to your most important point. If you ask for *information,* you may need to indicate how the information will be used. When you *order* something, you may need to explain how you will use what you order. When you send an *invitation,* you should explain all the circumstances that will occur if the person accepts the invitation.

3. *Closure.* Offer a clear statement of the action you seek. This statement will often echo the main point of your preparation section. Such repetition keeps your main point focused in your reader's mind after the person has grasped the details and explanation of your expansion section. If you want your order by a certain date, you might want to say "Please ship my order for 500 mixed-color bal-

---

REQUESTS

Preparation:
> State clearly what you want, why you want it, and (if needed) who wants it.

Expansion:
> Make only one point in each paragraph.
> Arrange points in order of priority (beginning with or leading to most important points) or in the order they will be best understood by the reader.

Closure:
> Clearly state the action you seek.
> Say something positive or friendly, if appropriate.

loons collect via UPS so that they will reach me by October 14." As part of your closure, you may also wish to say something positive or friendly to your reader.

Consider the following *requests:*

1212 Cedar
Jacksonville, LA 23701
July 10, 1984

Dr. Ellen James
Dean of Students
Western University
Jacksonville, LA 23707

Dear Dr. James:

Will you please send me a list of scholarships available this fall?

As a senior, I have a G.P.A. of 3.75 in the School of Business, with a concentration in Finance and Property Management. However, my plan to graduate in June 1985 depends upon whether I am able to get the funds to attend school this fall. Because I was unable to get the job I had hoped for this summer and because all funds from Financial Aid have been allocated for next year, I will not have enough money to pay for fall registration, housing, and books. A scholarship will help defray these costs.

Since, the fall quarter begins soon, I would greatly appreciate receiving the list of scholarships as soon as possible, along with information about how and when to apply.

Sincerely,

Jane Meyer

1. Does the first paragraph clearly indicate what the writer wants? The first paragraph is only a single short sentence. Should it be expanded?

2. The entire expansion section is one paragraph. Should the paragraph be divided? Should another be added?
3. Does the writer clearly indicate the action she seeks?

123 Hemlock Hall
Sylvan State University
Finger Lake, NY 20223
February 14, 1984

Mr. George Lewis
Director of Research and Development
Sundown-Cascade Company
650 Long Flume Blvd.
Big Timber, WA 98456

Dear Mr. Lewis:

To complete my senior thesis in forestry, I would like to obtain current information about your company's recently developed "Supergrow" variety of Douglas fir.

My senior thesis focuses on the ways in which genetically superior, rapidly growing varieties of conifers can contribute to increased yields in a range of climatic and geographical conditions. I plan to compare the advantages of the most prominent of the new varieties, concentrating on growth rates, fiber strength, resistance to disease, and estimated costs per thousand board feet.

From my major professor, Dr. Rolf Monteen, and from reading current periodicals, I understand that the "Supergrow" Douglas fir promises to develop at nearly twice the normal rate and appears highly resistant to disease. However, all the information I can obtain locally is at least two years old, and most of that information is too general to provide the details I need for my study.

I would appreciate receiving any reports or data that your company has assembled on the "Supergrow" tree. My thesis will be used only to meet a requirement for my degree and will not be published. I would be happy to send you a copy when it is complete; it is due on April 25. I would also appreciate receiving any related information you might have available, including the names of particular researchers I might contact.

Sincerely,

Paul Murphy

1. Does the first paragraph clearly indicate what the writer wants? In this paragraph, should the writer be more specific about what he needs?
2. What is the purpose of paragraphs 2 and 3? What would be the effect of reversing their order?
3. Does the writer clearly state the action he seeks?

COMPLAINTS

A *complaint* is not a chance to express annoyance about something or an excuse to let off steam, but a communication designed to rectify an error. If Acme Animal Exchange sends you a gorilla instead of a panda or if Gobble Oil Company's computers overbill you by $3000, you might write a letter of complaint. (Your first reaction might be to reach for the telephone, but you would then have no paper trail for legal purposes and would probably have trouble finding someone to correct the problem anyway. For significant matters, written communication usually straightens out problems most effectively.)

A *complaint* tries to achieve a specific result. Because someone has probably made an unintentional error, you can assume that if you explain the problem and how you want it rectified, the person reading your letter will do what you ask. Nastiness has no place in a complaint, and the person who reads your letter will probably not be the one who made the error. Concentrate instead on explaining the error and any circumstances the reader might need to know to act on your complaint.

A Design for Complaints

1. *Preparation.* In your opening paragraph, *identify* (do not explain) the problem and *what you want done* about it. Did you

receive 500 rubber cigars instead of 500 mixed-color balloons you ordered? Tell the company that it "shipped the wrong merchandise." To help the person who must straighten out the mess, refer to any invoice numbers, dates, model numbers, or whatever else will get the reader to the appropriate paperwork. Then indicate what you want (money back? the balloons? the cigars plus a partial refund?).

2. *Expansion.* While you simply identified the problem in the *preparation* section, you may *explain* the whole situation in the *expansion* section. What does the reader need to know about the problem? What else might help the reader take the action you seek? After you isolate each point you wish to make about the problem, make those points in individual paragraphs. Use either time or order of importance to arrange your paragraphs.

Suppose, for example, that after a month a home videogame you bought by mail quit working when you put in a new cartridge. You would need to explain precisely the circumstances of the failure. You might devote one paragraph to what happened when the failure occurred (including any early warnings that something might be wrong), a paragraph explaining what you tried to do after the problem developed, and a paragraph explaining the symptoms you have observed.

The *expansion* section explains whatever needs to be said about the problem to make the reader fully understand it and feel ready to take action. Instead of having to send back your home videogame,

---

COMPLAINTS

Preparation:
  Identify the problem, but don't explain it.
  Indicate what you want done about the problem.
Expansion:
  Tell the reader what her or she needs to know about the problem.
  Make only one point in a paragraph.
  Use time or order of importance to arrange your paragraphs.
Closure:
  Clearly indicate the specific action or adjustment you want.

you might be able to take care of the problem yourself if you explain the situation so clearly that a technician can recognize the problem and offer a solution (e.g., clean "terminal A"). If the suggestions works, both you and the company will be spared expense and trouble. If you suffer considerable inconvenience from a broken-down product, explain carefully the inconvenience and how the company might alleviate it. Make your explanation reasonable and unthreatening, with facts and details clarifying the problem and leading to the course of action you seek.

3. *Closure.* Indicate the specific action or adjustment that you want, making certain to state your request clearly and unambiguously. If you want the 500 balloons by October 15 and you are unwilling to accept them after that date, say so.

Here is a sample *complaint:*

> 1010 Marsh Street
> Livermore, KA 67831
> May 11, 1984

Mr. Harry M. Fitzsimmons
Customer Service Manager
Transnational Bus Company
120 East Street
Slackville, KA 67771

Dear Mr. Fitzsimmons:

You will be interested, I think, in the experience I had April 15, traveling on your company's bus from Livermore to Slackville. Since the bus driver left me stranded at an unscheduled stop, I believe I am entitled to a partial refund of the $37 fare.

The bus I took at 6:20 A.M. was scheduled to make four stops along the way and to arrive in Slackville at 12:15 P.M. I was scheduled to speak at 1 P.M. to the Governor's Commission on Disaster Preparations; therefore it was imperative that I be in Slackville no later than 12:30 P.M.

At about 10:30 A.M., after making four scheduled stops, the driver made an unscheduled stop at a café about a half-mile from the freeway near King City. He told the passengers we would have time to stretch and have a cup of coffee. After drinking my coffee, I stepped into the restroom to wash my hands. When I came outside, about three minutes later, the bus was gone. The driver apparently left without a warning and without counting his passengers.

The café's owner said that twice during the past month the same driver had stranded passengers. When I explained the importance of my speech, the owner of the café fortunately offered to drive me in her car to catch up with the bus. We thought we could catch the bus within a few miles, but the bus went so fast that we didn't catch it until the next scheduled stop, which was thirty miles later in Houghton. When I got on the bus, the driver neither apologized nor explained why he left the café so hurriedly and without warning.

Since I gave the café's owner ten dollars to cover her expenses, did not ride the bus for thirty miles of the trip, and was upset and inconvenienced by the experience, I would like a partial refund of my fare.

Sincerely,

James Stacey

1. How does the writer choose to identify the problem? What does he indicate he wants done?
2. Identify the key point of each paragraph.
3. What is the reason for ordering paragraphs 2, 3, and 4 as they are now ordered?
4. Does the final paragraph indicate clearly what the writer wants? Should the writer be more specific about the amount he thinks would be fair?

GOOD NEWS MESSAGES

It is always easy to tell people what you know they want to hear. A *good news message* can be sent whenever a reader will appreciate what you say: when you accept an invitation, immediately clear up a problem presented in a complaint letter, send along information someone requests, or thank someone for an order. Even though you may not feel entirely good about the news you send (you dislike the president of the school where you agreed to speak or you suspect the customer caused a product to break down while under warranty), you can focus on the good news. No one will gain if you express reservations that don't affect your actions.

A Design for Good News Messages

1. *Preparation.* The main point of a good news message is the news that will most please the reader. That main point should be expressed in the first paragraph (in the first sentence, if possible), pleasing the reader from the beginning and setting the tone for the message. If you have cleared up a $3000 computer error overcharging someone, tell the reader that right away. Remember, though, to think of your good news in terms of what the reader will consider good news. If you are a retailer and a customer has asked to have his home videogame reparied or replaced, the best news will not be that the manufacturer has agreed to reimburse you (the retailer) for the full repair cost. (That is probably good news for you, though.) But the good news for the customer is that you will repair the game without charge and return it within five days. Why would the customer worry about whether you get paid back? That is outside the customer's scope of concern. He wants to know about the answer to his problem.

2. *Expansion.* Develop in detail anything that clarifies the good news and that emphasizes positive qualities about the product, service, or company. Usually you will first want to explain the good news in detail, point by point. If the home videogame needs to be sent to your shop for repair, explain how it should be shipped.

Once you spell out the good news, you might remind the person of other services or products you offer, or you might say something positive that will create good will for your organization. If you have accepted an invitation to speak, you might, for example, say something about a positive experience you had in the past with the organization before which you will speak.

3. *Closure.* The ending of a good news message will often be more chatty than substantial. Repeat briefly the good news ("I look forward to speaking to Whitman's graduating class on June 11" or "You may expect your home videogame within three days after it reaches

---

GOOD NEWS MESSAGES

Preparation:
> *State the best news immediately in the first paragraph.*
> *Be certain that you present what the reader will consider the best news.*

Expansion:
> *Explain the good news in detail, one point per paragraph.*
> *Offer other positive comments about your organization, as appropriate.*

Closure:
> *Briefly repeat the good news.*
> *Provide friendly comments, as appropriate.*

---

our shop"). Typically such messages end with such formalities as thanks or offers to help in the future.

Here is a *good news message:*

TRANSNATIONAL BUS COMPANY

120 East Street
Slackville, KA 67771

May 18, 1984

Mr. James Stacey
1010 Marsh Street
Livermore, KA 67831

Dear Mr. Stacey:

Thank you for letting us know about your recent experience on a Transnational bus to Slackville. Enclosed is a check for $37, representing a full refund of your round-trip ticket.

Transnational is proud of its reputation for prompt and reliable service, and we constantly strive to improve. We appreciate hearing about problems so that we can correct them quickly. We want you to know that this is the first time that we have been notified about a passenger being stranded at an unscheduled stop.

The safety of our passengers is very important to us, and we have a strict company policy forbidding unscheduled stops except for emergencies. In addition, the driver is supposed to count the passengers before reboarding should an unscheduled stop be necessary. Please accept our sincere apologies for your inconvenience.

Bob Johnson is normally one of our most dependable drivers. He explained that the distance between stops four and five on the Slackville route is so long that passengers appreciate the chance to get our and stretch their legs briefly. For the convenience of our passengers, we are considering adding a scheduled stop in the King City area.

Again, thank you for taking the time to tell us about this matter. We want to provide all our passengers with the very best transportation service. We hope our apologies and refund will compensate for your inconvenience. We look forward to putting you back on our list of satisfied customers.

Sincerely yours,

Harry M. Fitzsimmons
Customer Service Manager

BAD NEWS MESSAGES

We all know the feeling of having to pass on bad news. It's never easy. An effective bad news message delivers the unwelcomed news gently and reasonably. What if you cannot comply with a request in a complaint letter (the person actually ordered 500 rubber cigars by mistake rather than 500 balloons—you have a photo copy of the original order—and your supply of balloons is exhausted), you cannot accept an invitation, you must refuse credit, or you cannot send the information that the person requested? Sometimes you can convey the bad news directly, stating the bad news in the first paragraph just as you would state good news. In most cases, though, you will find it more effective to withhold the bad news until you have cushioned its impact. A bad news letter therefore relies on an *indirect* design. You avoid the key issue until you prepare your reader for the bad news.

A Design for Bad News Messages

1. *Preparation.* The opening should serve as a cushion preparing for the bad news. (The bad news will be buried in the *expansion* section.) The cushion should be on the topic but should avoid the bad news. By the end of the first paragraph, the reader should not know, by tone or statement, what the news will be.

Here are some typical approaches used to create a cushion:

a. Thank the reader for something (for inviting you to speak, for interest in your company).
b. Compliment the person (on having a history of good credit or on representing a school with a strong reputation and from which your company regularly recruits employees).
c. Agree on some point with your reader (she should expect her home videogame to last at least three years without needing repair).
d. Find some related good news to make contact.

2. *Expansion.* Point by point, review the circumstances of the situation and lead to a stated or implied conclusion (the bad news). First, *review* all the facts of the situation, and then, if necessary, *analyze* the facts. An indirect approach uses inductive reasoning: you present the explanation piece by piece until you lead to the inevitable conclusion (the bad news). Often reviewing the facts requires using *time* as a basis for organizing; if so, look for logical divisions of time for paragraph breaks. Short, logical paragraphs will help make your explanation seem reasonable to your reader.

By withholding the bad news, you let your reader first see a reasonable explanation for why you must do something the reader will not like. If you do your work well, the reader will agree with you. If you leave out something important, you will probably hear from the person again.

It is important to remain factual when writing a bad news message. Accusing your reader directly of lying or of mistreating a product will create anger even if you are right. It is better to explain the facts as you see them than to make judgments about the person to whom you write.

BAD NEWS MESSAGES

Preparation:

   *Instead of stating your main point, provide a cushion that is
      on the topic but avoids the bad news.*

Expansion:

   *Review the facts of the situation. Usually time will provide a
      basis for organizing.*

   Analyze those facts, as appropriate.

   *Imply or state directly the bad news, but place it where it will
      not be emphasized.*

Closure:

   Say something positive.

   Do not mention the bad news.

3. *Closure.* Although it may be difficult, find something positive to say in your final paragraph ("I would be pleased to speak at your school next year" or "Our new line of home video machines has been designed to prevent jamming and carries a five-year guarantee; we would be pleased to accept your present unit for a trade-in at full retail value"). The closure should avoid mention of the bad news.

Here is a *bad news message* that was sent to a regular customer who angrily insisted that the company replace a clothes dryer that stopped running after only six months:

Rinso Appliance Company
1234 Flat Street
Springfield, IL 62301
September 1, 1984

Mr. Larry Miller
121 Pipe Lane
Rantoul, IL 61403

Dear Mr. Miller:

You are certainly right in saying that your Rinso clothes dryer should have held up longer than it did. Rinso dryers normally last at least ten years under normal conditions.

Mr. Roger Fixet, the manager of Rantoul Appliances where you bought your dryer, arranged to send your dryer on our truck's return trip from our last delivery to Rantoul Appliances. The dryer arrived at our service center yesterday. I immediately asked our best repairman to inspect your dryer, and I then inspected the machine personally to make certain that his diagnosis was correct.

Our inspection confirmed the burned-out motor reported by Mr. Fixet. Since our motors rarely burn out and since you have used your dryer for only six months, we inspected the motor carefully for defects. Although we found no signs of defects, the condition of the brushes in the motor indicate that the motor has severely overheated. Since all lubricants and seals are intact, the overheating could only have been caused by placing a sustained overload on the motor. Continued overheating eventually caused the motor to fail.

Because our preliminary diagnosis indicated that overloading caused the motor to fail, we inspected closely the dryer's drum, concentrating especially on the point at which the metal drum rides on the nylon-coated support just above the door. The nylon was deeply scored. Such scoring further indicates that the dryer has been consistently overloaded during use. The instructions accompanying the dryer state that no more than twelve pounds of clothing should be dried at one time. In addition, every Rinso dryer comes with a bright red lable warning users not to dry more than twelve pounds in a load.

The Rinso dryer has always been top-rated by *Consumer's Report* as well as by other consumer magazines that test home appliances independently. We have tremendous faith in Rinso's quality. To demonstrate this faith to you, we will put your machine in perfect working order for the cost of replacement parts only. There will be no charge for the labor involved or for Mr. Fixet's service call. These two expenses alone normally run about $65. The cost for replacing your dryer's motor and the nylon-coated support will be only $55.

To return your dryer to you within four days, I will need your approval to make the necessary repairs. The machine will then be as good as new and will still carry the original two-year guarantee. Please return the enclosed card indicating your approval. If you have further questions, please call me at 337/525-1212.

Sincerely,

Nancy Lucas
Manager

1. Identify the cushion. What is its tone? What are the advantages to this cushion?
2. What is the basis of organization for paragraphs 2, 3, and 4? What does the writer hope to accomplish in these paragraphs?
3. Why is paragraph 5 placed after paragraph 4? What would be the advantages or disadvantages of placing paragraph 5 after paragraph 1?
4. In what way is the bad news indicated? What might be the effect of stating the bad news directly?
5. What does the last paragraph try to accomplish?

RESEARCH REPORTS

Most research reports follow a basic design familiar to those who write and read such reports. We include the following design to show a fixed design structuring a long discourse; while most students are unlikely to use such a design in a composition course, they are likely to write research reports in other college classes. This design will work for a variety of situations (lab reports, feasibility studies, sociological investigations), but scientific or technical studies most suit it. Like all designs, it must sometimes be adapted, although the design follows a plan common in both school and industry.

A Design for Research Reports
1. *Preparation.* Explain the *purpose, method,* and *scope* of your work clearly enough to orient your reader, but do not bog down your

reader in specifics. Depending on the length and purpose of the report, you might need to include *background* (anything about the history of the project that will help your reader to understand what you are doing), or you may provide *a list of subtopics*, spelling out the major sections into which you have divided your report.

2. *Expansion.*

a. *Literature Review.* To show that you have done your homework on the problem (for the benefit of employer, professor, or client), you may need to summarize and review the professional literature on your subject. Your *literature review* should be kept relevant to the precise problem you are working on, should demonstrate your clear understanding of the problems encountered by others doing similar work, and should lead clearly to the present state of knowledge about the subject.

b. *Procedure.* Explain the procedure (or procedures) used to solve the problem. If the procedure is standard, simply name it. If you believe your reader will benefit from some knowledge of the procedure, summarize it. If your procedure is unusual or invented for the particular project, describe it in detail.

c. *Equipment and Materials.* If appropriate, describe the equipment and materials (in some cases facilities as well) used in your work. You will need to provide detailed description or discussion only if the equipment or materials are unusual.

d. *Results.* In this section, present a factual account of what happened in the course of your work. Sometimes results (especially for scientific work) are presented in list or graph form. Do not interpret results in this section. Present only the facts developed in carrying out your work.

e. *Discussion.* This is an important section since most readers care more about the implications of your work than about its details. Readers who are untrained will have trouble making sense of the facts you present in your section on results, but they will look for a narrative making sense of those results. In addition to explaining and evaluating the results, the discussion section points out their limitation, accounts for whatever is unexpected, and reveals any suspicions you have of error. By the end of the discussion, the reader should be clear about the significance of your findings. Many reports do not separate the *results* and *discussion* sections, but place any data that are clearly technical in an appendix and focus on explaining the results.

3. *Closure.* The *closure* for a research report is really another two sections of the report (sometimes combined) that focus the rest of the report on what the writer can conclude and on what he or she can recommend based on those conclusions.

a. *Conclusions.* Although conclusions are often drawn, or at least inferred, in the various sections of the discussion, many writers like to place conclusions in summary form after the discussion. Sometimes the conclusions are offered in numerically separated sentences so that a reader can clearly see that the writer draws, for example, seven specific and separately identifiable conclusions from his work. All conclusions must be drawn directly from what has gone before, especially from the *discussion.* Regardless of whether something undiscussed is interesting or true, it does not belong in the conclusion section unless thoroughly covered in the discussion.

b. *Recommendations.* Once you have drawn conclusions, you will be ready in some cases to offer specific suggestions for action in your *recommendations.* As with conclusions, recommendations are often presented in list form so that each stands out as a specific and separate possibility. Some reports include recommendations with conclu-

---

RESEARCH REPORTS

Preparation:
> Orient your reader to the purpose, method, and scope of your work.
> Include any necessary background.
> Provide a list of subtopics, if appropriate.

Expansion:
> Review the literature on the subject.
> Explain the procedure(s) used to solve the problem.
> Describe the equipment and materials used.
> Present your results.
> Discuss the implications of your results.

Closure:
> Present your conclusions.
> Present your recommendations, if appropriate.

sions, some with discussion, and some alone. The recommendations often parallel the conclusions, which seems logical since the recommendations are based directly on the conclusions. However, not all reports call for recommendations. Provide them only when the situation warrants doing so.

As reports become elaborate, they take on additional parts (e.g., an introductory summary or abstract and a table of contents). The design will, however, furnish you with a sense of structure to apply to any scientifically oriented report you must do.

The following research report is typical of those presenting scientific research, although much shorter than most. (Research reports are usually both longer than this sample and are written in ways that are difficult for a layperson to understand.) This report begins with an abstract—a summary of the report—and then spends the first three paragraphs providing purpose, method, scope, background, and a review of pertinent literature. (The literature review in this case is short—referring the reader to specific sources—and is included with the introduction.) Paragraphs 4 through 7 explain the experimenters' procedures, paragraph 5 (including the table and figure) presents the results, and the remainder of the report discusses those results, with the last paragraph furnishing a conclusion. Recommendations would be inappropriate to this report. As you read this report, notice the way in which the writers compare the two types of bees. (See p. 115 for a discussion of comparison and contrast.)

COLONY DEFENSE BY AFRICANIZED AND EUROPEAN HONEY BEES*

ABSTRACT

Africanized and European honey bee (Apis mellifera) populations showed quantitative differences in colony defensive behavior. Africanized bees responded faster and in much larger numbers than European honey bees and produced 8.2 and 5.9 times as many stings during two different experiments. Times to react to alarming

*Throughout the report, the numbers in parentheses refer to source notes that are not shown here. Note also that there are references to a table and figure that have not been reproduced here.

*stimuli were negatively correlated with the number of bees respond-
ing and to the total number of stings. The number of bees responding was significantly correlated to the total number of stings only for
the Africanized population.*

By 1990 *(1)*, American agriculture may have to deal with the
immigration of the Africanized bee, an insect with the potential
to alter agricultural practices and significantly increase the
cost of bee-pollinated food products. Honey bees *(Apis mellifera)* are not native to the Western Hemisphere, but were
introduced to the Americas through importations of European
stocks (*A. m. mellifera* and *A. m. ligustica*) since 1621 *(2)*. In
1956, a variety from Africa, *A. m. scutellata* (formerly *adan-
sonii*) *(3)*, was introduced into Brazil for the purpose of
improving honey production with a more tropically adapted
bee *(4)*. The variety of honey bee resulting from the inter-
breeding of the established European and newly imported Afri-
can types, referred to as the Africanized bee, has spread
through much of South America and into Panama.

The Africanized bee has received considerable coverage in
the popular press, from early stories about hoards of bees
stinging victims to death and the subsequent "killer bee" label
to more recent reports from Brazil that the bees are no longer
a problem. The tendency to sting readily is the most objection-
able characteristic of Africanized bees, one that is shared by
the parental *A. m. scutellata* in South Africa *(5)*. However, scientific data on stinging behavior of Africanized bees is limited
(6–9), and there are none dealing with the stinging behavior
of Africanized bees from the population in northern South
America which is spreading toward the United States.

Stinging is only one possible final behavior in a sequence of
acts by a honey bee that are collectively called defensive
behavior *(10)*. As part of our assessment of the potential
impact of the Africanized bee on the American beekeeping
industry, we quantified differences in defensive behavior,
especially stinging, between European and Africanized honey
bee populations.

Experiment I involved 150 large colonies in Baton Rouge,
Louisiana, and 147 similar-sized colonies in Monagas, Venezuela. The Louisana colonies had been established from various U.S. commercial honey bee stocks. The Venezuelan col-

onies had once contained European bees but were chosen on the basis that they had been allowed to breed freely for at least the past year with the feral Africanized bees which had been in the area for at least 2 years. All the hive entrances were made uniform (14 by 1.5 cm), and any additional openings were screened shut.

For experiment 2, 15 colonies of Africanized bees and 15 colonies of European bees were used. The colonies were equalized so that each consisted of 900 g of bees on three (43 by 20 cm) combs in new 20-liter hives, with entrances 3 cm in diameter. These colonies were established at a single location near Maturin, Monagas, Venezuela.

Each colony was tested twice in a standard, 90-second test sequence (II). Observations of defensive behavior were quantified in three ways (i) The number of bees at the colony entrance was counted from photographs taken at 30-second intervals during the test. (ii) Two time measurements were made: the length of time until bees began to emerge after alarm pheromone was sprayed above the entrance, and the length of time it took the first bee to orient to and on a moving target in front of the colony. (iii) The number of stings in the suede leather targets was counted.

An important consideration in evaluating colony defensive behavior is the temperature and relative humidity at the time of testing (4, 12, 13). The conditions during measurement of the Louisiana population (temperature, 25° to 36°C; relative humidity, 61 to 97 percent) were very similar to those in Venezuela (temperature, 26° to 35°C; relative humidity, 61 to 92 percent). In experiment 2, bees were tested at one location and thus were in similar environments.

Means ± standard error (S.E.) for the seven measures of defensive behavior are shown in Fig. 1 [not shown]. Differences were determined by a one-way analysis of variance on log-transformed data. In both experiments, the Africanized bees responded more quickly to both pheromone and targets. In most instances during experiment 1, the responses of Africanized bees to the targets were immediate, and occasionally the targets were stung before they were placed at the entrance. This was in marked contrast to the European colonies where many bees continued to forage and did not respond at all.

In experiment 1, the Africanized colonies had significantly

greater numbers of bees at the entrance at all times than the European colonies had. However, the numbers reported for the Africanized bees at the entrance were often underestimates of the numbers of bees responding, because immediately after the pheromone spraying many of these bees became airborne. In contrast, the European bees usually remained near the entrance until the targets provided a stimulus for orientation and attack.

The small colonies in experiment 2 had very few bees at the entrance at any time. The Africanized bees that did respond tended to fly away from the entrance, especially in the presence of a moving target, and thus were not included in the picture counts. These two conditions could explain the lack of a significant difference between the two populations for the preliminary (pre) and 90-second counts.

The total number of stings recorded from the large Africanized colonies of experiment 1 averaged 8.2 times greater than that recorded from European colonies and from the smaller colonies of experiment 2, averaged 5.9 times greater. However, the total number of stings produced by the Africanized bees in experiment 1 was probably an underestimation, especially for the most responsive colonies, because the targets were completely covered by bees within a few seconds of being presented. Since the bees remained on the targets (biting and stinging), other bees could not reach the surface with their stings.

Correlations between measures of all traits are presented in Table 1 [not shown]. Among the significant correlations, times to react were negatively correlated with numbers of bees and stings and positively correlated with each other, as would be expected. Bee counts and stings were positively correlated. A few correlations were not significant in one population, but significant for the other. The most notable differences were nonsignificant correlations in the European population between time to react to pheromone and either time to react to target or total number of stings, and between number of bees in pre, 30-second, and 60-second pictures and the total number of stings. These correlations were significant for the Africanized population. This difference reflects a greater proportion of Africanized bees participating in colony defense, as compared with European bees.

Other differences apparent in the responses showed by the

two populations were not quantified in the test. The most obvious of these was the propensity for the Africanized bees to come out of the colony and fly. There were many more bees in the air and harassing the experimenters during tests of these colonies than during tests of the European colonies. In addition, Africanized bees at the entrance frequently attacked other bees—a behavior not exhibited by the European bees.

The number of stings in a leather ball was measured on colonies of bees in Brazil under temperature conditions (24° to 32°C) similar to those of our study *(12)*. With adjustments for different target sizes, Africanized bees in northern and southern Brazil stung at rates of 0.32 and 0.26 stings per square centimeter in 30 seconds, respectively, whereas the Venezuelan population we studied averaged 0.85 stings per square centimeter in 30 seconds. This refutes the idea that the migrating bees have become milder through hybridization with "native" bees.

The measures of defensive behavior made during our studies indicate that the Africanized bee as it currently exists in Venezuela is significantly different from its European counterpart in the United States. The Africanized bees respond to colony disturbance more quickly, in greater numbers, and with more stinging. The impact of such a bee on the U.S. beekeeping industry and agriculture would be considerable. Public response to the possibility of severe stinging and death would cause many beekeepers to give up beekeeping or reduce their colony holdings. The resulting reduction in honey production, and the loss of the major insect pollinator of many crops, would constitute a major expense for American agriculture.

—Anita M. Collins, Thomas E. Rinderer, John R. Harbo, and
Alan B. Bolten

EXERCISES

1. As chairperson of your school's Commencement Committee, you must invite a speaker for June's graduation ceremony. The committee's first choice is one of your state's senators. Write to the senator inviting him or her to speak.
2. Assume that you plan to attend a small college that is over a thousand miles from your home. The college has no dormitory facilities and tells all its new students to write directly to a local rental agency for housing information.

Write to the agency to find out what is available. Make sure that you explain your particular circumstances so that the agency can provide you with specific help. (You might mention the amount you can spend a month, transportation needs, whether you prefer roommates or living alone, the number of months per year you expect to live there, and any special considerations you have.)

3. On your way back to college after Christmas vacation, Sky High Airlines lost your luggage. The luggage was a Christmas gift from your grandparents, and your grandparents still have the receipts. Not only were your clothes lost, but also your textbooks and two term papers that were nearly completed. For the past three weeks you have repeatedly called the local agent who has begrudgingly agreed, after all your phone calls, to replace the luggage with a set costing less than half the set you lost. He has refused all compensation for the contents of the suitcase. Write a letter to the company's president, J. B. Pilote, at the corporate headquarters in Chicago, Illinois, seeking whatever adjustment you think is appropriate.

4. The day after you bought a new stereo from Sunshine Sound, the company closed and filed for bankruptcy. Four days later, the stereo quit working. Since no other company in your area carries the same brand, you have not been able to find another dealer within driving distance who will honor the one-year warranty. Write to the manufacturer to rectify the situation.

5. Adopt the role of the person to whom you wrote in Exercises 2, 3, 4, or 5 and answer the letter you wrote with good news.

6. Adopt the role of the person to whom you wrote in Exerises 2, 3, 4, or 5 and answer the letter with bad news.

7. Someone made a mistake in scheduling the Special Olympics at your school. The October date was not cleared properly, and not only is that date unavailable but no date or place can be found until April. It is now September 15, and all other plans have been made and all participants have made arrangements to attend. Some people planned to come from as far away as a hundred miles. As chairperson of the event, you must notify the directors of each of the thirty groups planning to bring participants that the October meet must be canceled. Write the letter.

The Flexible Designs

Fixed designs serve well-defined needs for well-defined readers. As the word "flexibility" implies, *flexible designs* function for a broad range of writing contexts. The rise of fixed designs came primarily through the specialized needs of science, business, and industry, especially in the past fifty years. Most of the flexible designs, on the other hand, have been with us for over two thousand years. The flexible designs are so ingrained in our communication that it is impossible to avoid them when using the fixed designs.

Both kinds of design share a three-part structure: *prepare* the reader; *expand* the purpose identified in the preparation section; and *close* by making certain that the purpose has been achieved. But what goes in each section can be identified much more specifically for fixed designs than for flexible designs. Predictably, fixed designs are much more recognizable. A person knows that he or she is reading a fixed design, whereas flexible designs often seem invisible. In actuality, both demand careful structuring, but the writer using fixed designs works less hard to organize than does the writer using only flexible designs.

Good design allows the reader to focus on content. The formalities of the design "disappear" since good design does not draw attention to itself. The formal features are there, but the reader does not notice them. An analogy can be found in the basic unit of language, the sentence. As long as a writer follows the rules for constructing sentences (grammar and syntax), no one notices. Let's try that again. As lung the constructing for a writer sentences (grammer an sintaxes) follow, one no note is. Get the point? We only notice form when it confuses us. Good design lets readers focus on content and prevents awkwardness from distracting them. As Ovid said, "All art lies in concealing art."

As with fixed designs, flexible designs have developed for handling certain kinds of writing tasks. These designs can be placed in four categories: *describing objects, narrating events, explaining concepts,* and *arguing policies.* As you will see, though, these are really less categories than levels of thinking, each of which uses the categories below it. A writer needs description and narration to explain concepts, and all three contribute to argument. The following sections explain each of these kinds of writing and suggest designs suitable for the sort of writing you are likely to do.

DESCRIBING OBJECTS

Children learn at an early age to describe objects by color, size, and shape as well as to recognize objects resembling each other. Their simple descriptions, like ours, often start with "It looks like . . ." and then fill in other physical details. Descriptions tend to be visually oriented. Although we recall details of sound, smell, taste, and touch, most of what we want to describe or to hear described involves things we can see. In writing, the other senses are usually subordinated to sight.

Describing objects involves three elements:

1. *Characterizing physical traits.* Size, shape, texture, color, and other physical characteristics need to be sketched.
2. *Selecting a clear perspective.* The observer selects a particular position from which to view an object. That position should not be changed except for good reason and with fair warning to the reader. Depending on your purpose, you might choose to describe the radiator of a Rolls-Royce from a head-on perspective. Imagine your reader's confusion if you start with a head-on view, switch to an overhead view, return to head-on, change to inside the radiator, go back to head-on, switch to underneath, return to the inside, and end up on the engine side.
3. *Finding a recognizable order.* Just as you need to stick with the perspective you choose, details must be described systematically from your perspective. Often the order depends on the nature of the object, but some sort of order is usually apparent. The most common order is spatial (left to right, top to bottom). Other orders emphasize categories depending on size, shape, or function.

Consider the opening paragraph of Mark Twain's *Life on the Mississippi*:

The Mississippi is well worth reading about. It is not a commonplace river, but on the contrary is in all ways remarkable. Considering the Missouri its main branch, it is the longest river in the world—four thousand three hundred miles. It seems safe to say that it is also the crookedest river in the world, since in one part of its journey it uses up one thousand three hundred miles to cover the same ground that the crow would fly over in six hundred and seventy-five. It discharges three times as much water as the St. Lawrence, twenty-five times as much as the Rhine, and three hundred and thirty-eight times as much as the Thames. No other river has so vast a drainage-basin; it draws its water-supply from twenty-eight states and territories; from Delaware on the Atlantic seaboard, and from all the country between that and Idaho on the Pacific slope—a spread of forty-five degrees of longitude. The Mississippi receives and carries to the Gulf water from fifty-four subordinate rivers that are navigable by steamboats, and from some hundreds that are navigable by flats and keels. The area of its drainage-basin is as great as the combined areas of England, Wales, Scotland, Ireland, France, Spain, Portugal, Germany, Austria, Italy, and Turkey; and almost all this wide region is fertile; the Mississippi valley, proper, is exceptionally so.

Twain describes physical traits (length, shape, volume, sources), selects a clear perspective (a bird's-eye view), and finds a recognizable order (overview with dominant features, then moving from the drainage basin to the river's sources). Twain builds his description by *addition*, selecting and ordering details to suggest the river's massiveness through images of vast spaces and territories.

You will rarely be called on to write from such a lofty perspective. That is usually the task of a professional writing for a large audience. But you will be called on to provide descriptions for professors or employers. You might need to describe land that your company contemplates purchasing or organisms observed under a microscope during a laboratory experiment.

A warning, though: very few writers describe simply for the sake of description. There is almost always another motive. Usually a description contributes to a larger effort. The land you describe for your employer might be part of a feasibility study describing various parcels and then analyzing them in terms of your company's long-range plans. A lab report might describe what you saw under a microscope, but the report will probably focus on the significance of what was observed rather than on what was observed.

Keeping in mind that any description you write will probably contribute to a larger unit of writing, let us consider a design for writing a physical description.

A Design for Describing Objects

1. *Preparation.* First, *identify* the object and then provide an overview of it. Often the overview is achieved by comparing the object with other things. What is it like? Notice, for example, how Twain names the Mississippi and then places it among the rivers of the world. If it will help to orient the reader, you might want to list the segments as you will describe them. For example, you might say that you will describe the three major sections of the Mississippi River, beginning with its estuary, moving to the main river, and ending with the various rivers that feed into it.

2. *Expansion.* Describe each of the segments you have isolated, using the following pattern:

a. Identify the segment.
b. Provide any overview that might be needed.
c. Indicate the parts of the segment and then in order describe each, including whatever is important (texture, shape, size, material, etc.).

By subdividing and sub-subdividing the object into logical units, you can describe anything, regardless of its complexity, and still keep your reader oriented. The key here is to be certain that your segments are logical and that your reader will see that logic. If you describe a room, for example, you might treat each surface as a segment (four walls, a floor, and a ceiling, making six segments to describe).

3. *Closure.* Closure is less important in describing objects than in most other kinds of writing, primarily because description almost always exists in some context. Usually the description ends, and the writer goes on to deal with the significance of what was described. (See "Explaining Concepts.") You may simply end when you finish the description, you may provide a final overview, or you may restate the purpose if you pointed out one earlier.

DESCRIBING OBJECTS

Preparation:
   Identify and provide an overview of the object.
   List the segments of your description, if appropriate.
Expansion:
   Systematically describe each segment by identifying it, providing a useful overview, and describing the parts in order.
   Be certain that your segments are logically ordered and that your reader can see that logic.
Closure:
   You have three options: (1) simply end with description of the last segment, (2) provide a final overview, or (3) restate the purpose (if given).

This plan might not work for all situations calling for descriptive designs, but it will get you started. Its strength lies in dividing the subject into logical units that assure a complete description. Although this design seems to have the precision of a fixed design, it rarely forms a complete design—one that can stand alone. Each of the fixed designs specifies the arrangement for a complete discourse; the design for describing objects almost always is just one element contributing to a complete design, such as a report or an essay. While you may be asked to write a simple description as an exercise in a writing class, rarely will you encounter a circumstance in which your description stands alone.

The following is a brief description from a novel:

Identification and overview { This ball turret was a metal sphere with a glass porthole; it was set into the fuselage of a B-17 like a distended navel—like a nipple on the bomber's belly. In this tiny dome were two fifty-caliber machine guns and a short, small man whose chore was

Systematic description of segments { to track in his gunsights a fighter plane attacking his bomber. When the turret moved, the gunner revolved with it. There were wooden handles with buttons on the tops to fire the guns; gripping these trigger sticks, the ball turret gunner looked like some dangerous fetus suspended in the bomber's absurdly exposed amniotic sac, intent on protecting his mother. These handles also steered the turret—to a cut-off point, so that the ball turret gunner would not shoot off the props forward.

—John Irving, *The World According to Garp*

1. Point to the identification and to the precise words that provide an overview.
2. How does Irving organize the segments of this description?
3. For each segment, does he provide an identification and an overview?
4. This description comprises just over half a paragraph concentrating on the ball turret gunner, and the paragraph ends with this section. Does the description seem to have a specific closure?

The following is an example of a more sustained description:

During the time of the spring floods the best near view of the fall is obtained from Fern Ledge on the east side above the blinding spray at a height of about 400 feet above the base of the fall. A climb of about 1400 feet from the Valley has to be made, and there is no trail, but to any one fond of climbing this will make the ascent all the more delightful. A narrow part of the ledge extends to the side of the fall and back of it, enabling us to approach it as closely as we wish. When the afternoon sunshine is streaming through the throng of comets, ever wasting, ever renewed, the marvelous fineness, firmness, and variety of their forms are beautifully revealed.

At the top of the fall they seem to burst forth in irregular spurts from some grand, throbbing mountain heart. Now and then one mighty throb sends forth a mass of solid water into the free air far beyond the others, which rushes alone to the bottom of the fall with long streaming tail, like combed silk, while the others, descending in clusters, gradually mingle and lose their identity. But they all rush past us with amazing velocity and display of power, though apparently drowsy and deliberate in their movements when observed from a distance of a mile or two. The heads of these comet-like masses are composed of nearly solid water, and are dense white in color like pressed snow, from the friction they suffer in rushing through the air, the portion worn off forming the tail, between the white lustrous threads and films of which faint, grayish pencilings appear, while the outer, finer sprays of waterdust, whirling in sunny eddies, are pearly gray throughout.

At the bottom of the fall there is but little distinction of form visible. It is mostly a hissing, flashing, seething, upwhirling mass of scud and spray, through which the light sifts in gray and purple tones, while at times, when the sun strikes at the required angle, the whole wild and apparently lawless, stormy, striving mass is changed to brilliant rainbow hues, manifesting finest harmony.

The middle portion of the fall is the most openly beautiful; lower, the various forms into which the waters are wrought are more closely and voluminously veiled, while higher, towards the head, the current is comparatively simple and undivided. But even at the bottom, in the boiling clouds of spray, there is no confusion, while the rainbow light makes all divine, adding glorious beauty and peace to glorious power.

This noble fall has far the richest, as well as the most powerful, voice of all the falls of the Valley, its tones varying from the sharp hiss and rustle of the wind in the glossy leaves of the live oaks and the soft, sifting, hushing tones of the pines, to the loudest rush and roar of storm winds and thunder among the crags of the summit peaks. The low bass, booming, reverberating tones, heard under favorable circumstances five or six miles away, are formed by the dashing and exploding of heavy masses mixed with air upon two projecting ledges on the face of the cliff, the one on which we are standing and another about 200 feet above it. The torrent of massive comets is continuous at time of high water, while the explosive, booming notes are wildly intermittent, because, unless influenced by the wind, most of the heavier masses shoot out from the face of the precipice, and pass the ledges upon which at other times they are exploded.

Occasionally the whole fall is swayed away from the front of the cliff, then suddenly dashed flat against it, or vibrated from side to side like a pendulum, giving rise to endless variety of forms and sounds.

—John Muir, *Yosemite Falls*

1. Muir describes an object that is dynamic and changing. Does he face unique problems in describing the falls?
2. Why does he suggest that the falls be viewed from Fern Ledge?
3. In what ways does the first paragraph provide an overview?
4. How does Muir organize his expansion section? Why does he adopt such an order?
5. To which sense does Muir's description predominately appeal?
6. How might a scientific description of the falls differ from Muir's description?
7. What does Muir do to try to make the reader feel the effect of the falls upon a person standing on Fern Ledge?
8. What is the effect of Muir's closure?

EXERCISES

1. Because you are very familiar with a particular piece of land, you have been asked to describe that land for an environmental impact report. Write a description of the land that can be added to the report.
2. Think of a place you once knew well but that has been changed somehow (for example, a block or building that has now been torn down for urban renewal, an open area now covered with tract homes, or a beautiful place in the mountains that was destroyed by natural disaster). Since no pictures of the place exist, a local historical society has asked you to describe the place for its archives. In a letter to the society, describe the place.
3. The editor of the local paper is a friend of the head of the historical society in Exercise 2, and after hearing good reports about your letter to the society, she wants you to write a short feature article comparing how the place looks now with how it looked then. Write the article.
4. Several years ago you graduated from college. You now own a home and want to plant your first tree. You fondly remember a particular tree at the college, but since you now live a thousand miles away, you can't go there to find out what kind of tree it was. However, you still maintain contact with your English teacher, and you hope that she might be able to find out the information you need. In a

letter to the teacher, describe where the tree is and what it looks like. Make sure that you offer enough detail so that the teacher will have no trouble finding the location and that, if the tree has since been cut down, the teacher can read your description to the college's arborist to identify what kind of tree it was.

5. You have in mind a design for an arch over the main entrance to your college campus, but you can't draw well enough to make a face on a pumpkin. You briefly mentioned your idea to someone at a party, and the idea worked its way to the Campus Committee, which has been looking into designs for the arch. The committee's chairperson has sent you a note asking for a description of your design. Answer the request.

NARRATING EVENTS

Children also learn early to use chronology to tell about events. A child might say, "I went to the store, and then I got an ice cream cone, and then I got a cookie, and then I went home." *Narrating events* requires the ability to use time to order what happens. Although humans learn readily to recount events, most events can be seen at different levels of complexity. A child might see only four things in the day worth mentioning (store, ice cream cone, cookie, and home), but the parent accompanying the child will see the day much more minutely (galoshes on kids, coats on, kids fighting on their way to the car, heavy traffic, etc.). Humans obviously do not function like TV cameras, recording in the memory everything that passes before their eyes with the precise duration that events occur in life. Any time a person narrates events, orally or in writing, he or she selects and orders details for a listener or reader.

To narrate events is to present the past. A person rarely narrates events as they are happening. (Live television coverage provides the most obvious exception.) Consequently, narrative depends upon memory, and our memories store experience in categories based on connection and similarity, not on a simple chronology. One event reminds us of another, but not necessarily in chronological order. Memory is also selective. We forget much of what we experience unless we consciously and successfully choose what to remember.

Even then, we cannot be certain that the memory has not slipped. As a writer, always distrust your memory.

In some ways, *narrating events* depends upon a fixed design. Time orders the discourse. We feel comfortable with time because it structures much of our lives. Stories (events arranged in time) provide a common way of communicating. They help to entertain others, pass on information, or make a point. In other words, we have a purpose for narrating events, and that purpose governs the choice of what to say and of the amount of detail to include. While time provides the order of the details, the selection of those details challenges the writer. Let us look at a brief narrative:

> **One summer I started off to visit for the first time the city of Los Angeles. I was riding with some friends from the University of New Mexico. On the way we stopped briefly to roll an old tire into the Grand Canyon. While watching the tire bounce over tall pine trees, tear hell out of a mule train and disappear with a final grand leap into the inner gorge, I overheard the park ranger standing nearby say a few words about a place called Havasu, or Havasupai. A branch, it seemed, of the Grand Canyon.**
>
> **What I heard made me think that I should see Havasu immediately, before something went wrong somewhere. My friends said they would wait. So I went down into Havasu—fourteen miles by trail—and looked things over. When I returned five weeks later, I discovered that the others had gone on to Los Angeles without me.**
>
> **—Edward Abbey, *Desert Solitaire***

While Abbey's narrative covers five weeks, all sentences but the last focus on a small part of the first day. And Abbey leaves out most of the events of that day, concentrating instead on recounting the events that point out the impulsiveness of his decision. His purpose determines his selection of details.

Typical Narrative Applications

While narration includes storytelling in all its forms, most writers narrate events to report information, to explain or clarify an idea, or to persuade someone to accept a point. Because narrative can present interesting and poignant details, it is a useful tool when subordinated to a larger purpose. Let us look at a design for narrating events that assumes that you couple narration to a larger goal.

A Design for Narrating Events

1. *Preparation.* Let your reader know your *purpose* (why you are narrating the event) and your *perspective* (your relationship to the event). Often, both pieces of information can be passed on in a phrase. Notice, for example, how this middle section from a letter soliciting funds for Greenpeace makes clear the *purpose* and the *perspective* of the narrative:

> GREENPEACE is getting ready for the seal harvest just as it has for the last six years—by working on a way to stop it.
>
> Back in 1976, we began our campaign by trying to spray the pups with a harmless, organic dye (the dye would have made their pelts worthless to the hunters). In the years following, we have helped show some of the hunters how to earn their living *without* killing seals. And we not only went to the ice, we sent a secret investigative team out to prove who was making *the real* profits from the horrible slaughter. Last year GREENPEACE sent at tremendous cost its ship, the *Rainbow Warrior,* to take direct action against the hunt.
>
> The ship was seized and several GREENPEACE members were arrested for spraying the pups with the life-saving indelible green dye. With the help of residents of Prince Edward Island, GREENPEACE organized the protest to ban the hunt from the island. Bowing to pressure, *The Canadian government cancelled the "harvest" on PEI* with only 2,900 seal pups of the 10,000 quota captured. But—for all our efforts—the slaughter still goes on.

The first sentence prepares the reader by indicating that Greenpeace wants to stop the seal harvest (purpose) and that the organization has taken an active role in the past (perspective). The narrative represents a small part of a long appeal, with the narrative contributing to a larger purpose (to convince the reader to send funds supporting the efforts of Greenpeace to end the harvest of baby seals). The reader needs to know *why* he or she is asked to read the narration and to grasp *what* the writer's relationship to the events is. Sometimes that relationship is personal (as with Greenpeace), and sometimes it is disinterested.

2. *Expansion.* A narrative might be a single paragraph or pages long. If it is a paragraph, be sure to have events in correct order and to give enough attention to each event that your reader will grasp the *meaning* you want the narrative to convey. Treat longer narratives the same way, but look for divisions in time or development that will break the narrative into paragraphs. The challenge with narration lies less in being sure that you have events arranged properly in time than in making certain that you select detail effectively and allocate space in such a way that you say enough. Saying too little will leave your reader confused about the narrative's purpose; saying too much might get your reader so involved with the narrative that he or she will lose sight of your purpose. In the Greenpeace narrative, notice how time itself is less important than is establishing a track record of trying to do something about the problem.

3. *Closure.* Narratives end at the point in time that the writer decides the story is over, but usually the ending quickly follows the climax. Since narrative most often makes a point, the narrative stops when the point has been made. The purpose can be restated in other

---

NARRATING EVENTS

Preparation:
Identify your purpose and your perspective.
Expansion:
Tell the events in chronological order.
Select detail and allocate space so that your narrative will fulfill your purpose.
Closure:
Be certain that the point of your narrative is implicitly or explicitly clear.
Provide a transition to the next part of the discourse, if appropriate.

terms or the narrative can simply end. If the narrative contributes to a larger discourse, the writer returns to the discourse with a brief transition. Notice how the Greenpeace narrative ends with a transition that leads to a call for action about the problem. What "still goes on" demands attention.

The following paragraph uses narration to support a point:

Preparation { Young people spend a lot of time and energy trying to understand adult behavior and motivation and just how they fit into that world. Imagine what a young viewer of network TV must

Expansion { make of adult behavior on TV. On one evening he or she might see a comedy about people sharing an apartment arguing all the time and trying to be funny. This comedy is sure to be interrupted by commercials showing adults taking issues such as toilet paper and mouthwash very seriously. With only a minute's pause, a new program begins and the scene shifts to urban violence, also portraying people arguing and fighting—only this time there are no laughs. The violence is punctuated by several sports figures finger-wrestling and drinking beer or a number of attractive women draped across fancy cars. If the young viewers stay up late enough, they may even catch a bit of late-night news where an invasion is followed by a fashion show and a fire—all treated with the same seriousness or flip-

Closure { pancy, depending on the "personality" of the news crew. The segments of the programs follow each other so quickly and smoothly that, to a young mind, a battle in Asia and a fire in Chicago could be taking place next door to each other and most probably exist to them at the same level of reality as the detective story or situation comedy.

—Herbert Kohl

1. What is the purpose of this paragraph?
2. What is the perspective of the writer?
3. How does Kohl use chronological order in the expansion section?
4. How does the detail of the expansion section help to fulfill Kohl's purpose?
5. How does the closure make clear the point of the narrative?

The following short narrative is used in a long article explaining the great white shark:

> Drawing on my observations from a shark cage and information from scars on seals, as well as the shark's diet and interviews with attack victims, I have pieced together the following attack scenario. Imagine the cool coastal waters off California or southern Australia. An adult seal lies floating on its back, casually disrupting the surface water with its fin movements. (A hyperventilating skin diver may be substituted for the seal for the purpose of this discussion.) Thirty feet below, a 14-foot fish is cruising, gazing upward at the sea surface. The dark silhouette of the prey with light flickering at its edge visually attracts the shark. It turns and makes a rapid tail thrust, driving it surfaceward. The high-torque tail and stiff, fusiform body are propelled at 10 to 15 miles per hour.
>
> As the shark approaches to within about seven feet from its prey, it begins to extend its upper jaw upward and outward, lifting its snout and reducing its hydrodynamic posture but adding another few inches to its bite. Its eyes roll tailward in their sockets, exposing a white fibrous tissue that will protect the eyes should the prey attempt to damage them with its flipper nails. At this point, the shark cannot see the seal but relies instead on the electrical discharges it is receiving by sensors located on the underside of its now upturned snout. Simultaneously, the seal probably senses this onrushing predator and frantically tries to escape. In open water it could easily outmaneuver a white shark, but now it is faced with its own motionlessness as a ton of fish hurtles toward it. Some do escape, as is evidenced by the missing rear flippers and the incredible bite wounds on the haunches of elephant seals and southern fur seals off California and Australia.
>
> —John E. McCosker, "Great White Shark"

1. Identify the place where McCosker expresses his purpose.
2. Although this paragraph appears in a lengthy article where the writer's perspective is seen more fully, what indications do you see here of that perspective?
3. Point to the beginning and ending of the expansion sec-

tion. Why has McCosker selected the specific details presented in this section?

4. Does the closure make clear the point of the narrative?

EXERCISES

1. On your way back from Christmas vacation, you were arrested for speeding in a small town nearly two hundred miles away from your school. You do not believe that you were guilty, and the local judge has agreed to allow you to file a written deposition telling your side of the story since the distance from campus and the time away would clearly harm your studies. Write the deposition.

2. Your grandmother never went to college, but she thinks it is so important that you go that she has said she will give you a thousand dollars a year to help support you. You know she does not have a great deal of money, but because your education means so much to her, you have graciously accepted her offer. She only asks one thing: that you write a letter at the beginning of the year telling her what happened on your first day of classes. Tell her.

3. As a film and television reviewer for a small local newspaper, you are looking for something to review for next week's column. Together with the rest of your class, agree on a film or television program to review. Part of your review will be a four-hundred-word narrative telling what happened in the show. Write the narrative. (By having the whole class select the same show to review, you can later compare choices of selection of detail and allocation of space.)

4. An organization for which you work has asked you to help write a letter soliciting funds. You know that such letters often use short narratives because of the interest people have in poignant stories. In a separate statement, name the organization and tell the reader the effect you wish your narrative to have. Next, write the narrative that will go in the letter. Use the Greenpeace example on p. 90 as a model.

5. "What I did on my summer vacation" has long been the joke of writing assignments. Let's be brave and revive it. Write about one event from your summer vacation for each of the following contexts: a letter to a romantic partner from whom you have been separated for the summer,

a letter to your grandmother, a satiric narrative that is part of an article you are writing for your college newspaper.

6. Someday someone will write your obituary. Beat that person to it. Assume that you were killed while doing something that you enjoyed. Write your obituary, telling the readers of your hometown newspaper the public highlights of your life.

7. Select an important moment in history and describe that event from the perspective of a participant. Assume that your narrative will be part of that person's memoirs. Your narrative should differ in some ways from accepted historical versions.

8. Select a reader or group of readers to whom you would like to recount your proudest accomplishment or moment. Identify that reader (or group) and recount your accomplishment.

9. A biography of you has just been published, and you feel that it seriously misrepresents or distorts some important aspect of your life. Write a letter to the journal that recently published a review of the book setting the record straight.

Process Designs

While most narratives answer the question "What happened?" some answer the question "How is it done?" From winemaking to the way a jet engine creates thrust, people like to know how something happens. Because this kind of narrative shows up so often, it has its own name: *process*.

Process designs combine description and narration and, unlike other narratives, can frequently be explained in present tense. Processes are special events that recur, but that have definite beginnings and endings when they occur. A faucet gets a new washer, a pizza gets cooked. Some processes recount how something works to satisfy our curiosity (how an electron functions within an atom) and others tell us how to do something (balance a checkbook).

Let us look at one of each:

Let me describe how a friend of mine from a Rio Grande pueblo hunts. He is twenty-seven years old. The Pueblo Indians, and I think probably most of the other Indians of the Southwest,

begin their hunt, first, by purifying themselves. They take emetics, a sweat bath, and perhaps avoid their wife for a few days. They also try not to think certain thoughts. They go out hunting in an attitude of humility. They make sure that they need to hunt, that they are not hunting without necessity. Then they improvise a song while they are in the mountains. They sing aloud or hum to themselves while they are walking along. It is a song to the deer, asking the deer to be willing to die for them. They usually still-hunt, taking a place alongside a trail. The feeling is that you are not hunting the deer, the deer is coming to you; you make yourself available for the deer that will present itself to you, that has given itself to you. Then you shoot it. After you shoot it, you cut the head off and place the head facing east. You sprinkle corn meal in front of the mouth of the deer, and you pray to the deer, asking it to forgive you for having killed it, to understand that we all need to eat, and to please make a good report to the other deer spirits that he has been treated well. One finds this way of handling things and animals in all primitive cultures.

—Gary Snyder, *Turtle Island*

Every tent has its own stratagems for driving you to the brink of lunacy when you try to erect it in a high wind. But there are standard defensive measures with which you can counter. Before you unroll the tent itself and allow the wind to breathe berserk life into its billowing folds, have all the support weapons ready and waiting—poles, pegs, and an assortment of articles from pack or nature that are heavy enough to help hold down the wind-filled tent and yet smooth enough not to tear it. Then drive in the first peg, part way. For obvious reasons, wind- and door-wise, this peg should be the one for the center guy line of the foot end of the tent. If possible, hook this line over the peg before you unfold the tent. Drive the peg fully home, so that the line cannot by any devilish means flap free. Then take a deep breath and unfold the tent. Unfold it slowly, close to the ground, and onto each foot or so of unfolding fabric put one or more of the heavy, smooth articles. Their size and nature will depend on wind strength and campsite: sometimes all you can use is the full pack; big stones, when available, are godsends, but they must be smooth. Failing adequate heavy support weapons, sprawl yourself over the whistling, flapping bedlam. Slowly, painfully, drive in the pegs that hold down the edges of the stretched-out floor. If no stones are handy, drive in the pegs with your heels. Unless you've attempted this maneuver from the prone position in a thirty-mile-an-hour wind—brother, you haven't lived.

The sequence in which you tackle pole-erection and the securing of the other guy lines will depend on the structure of your tent and the vagaries of your temperament, but in general you fix the windward end first and you try to keep everything flat on the ground until you are ready to lift the fabric quickly into a taut, unflappable position. You can't possibly accomplish such an act, but you might as well aim for it. Once you've come anywhere close, your troubles are almost over. But if you get the tent up within double the time you figured on, count yourself a candidate for the Tent of Fame.

Once the tent is up you should check several times that no pegs are threatening to pull out. And, because even the tautest tent will flap in a high wind, you may have to tighten the lines occasionally. End-to-end stability is the most vital factor, and it pays to place the head-end peg so that the line tightener comes close to the apex of the tent and you can adjust it by simply reaching out from inside. If necessary, shorten the line by tying in a sheepshank.

—Colin Fletcher, *The Complete Walker*

The account of how Pueblo Indians hunt satisfies our curiosity about the process. Snyder assumes that we read out of interest, not to imitate. On the other hand, Fletcher's account of pitching a tent gives specific directions. Although written with humor, the narrative provides practical advice about how to complete the process. Both writers intend to recount a process, but they see readers using their narratives in quite different ways. Purpose affects the selection of detail, the allocation of space, and the way in which the writers address the readers.

Before starting to write a *process design,* clearly define for yourself the various steps required to complete the process. You and your reader will be confused if you back up because you left something out. Here is a basic plan that will work to describe most processes:

> ## PROCESSES
>
> ***Preparation:***
>   *Identify the process.*
>   *Provide useful overview.*
>   *List the steps, if appropriate.*
> ***Expansion:***
>   *Identify and provide an overview for each step.*
>   *Mention any special equipment or materials.*
>   *Explain the segments of each step.*
> ***Closure:***
>   *Summarize or provide an overview, if appropriate.*

A Design for Processes

1. *Preparation.* First, identify the process and then provide any overview that will help to orient your reader (such as where, when, or materials needed). It might then be helpful to provide a list of the steps needed to complete the process.

2. *Expansion.* Explain each step in order. Begin by identifying the step; then provide an overview of the step. (What does it contribute to the process?) If any special equipment or materials are needed, mention them. (For complex processes, you might need to repeat the procedure—identification, overview, materials, and description—for each segment and perhaps for each subsegment.)

3. *Closure.* Your narrative will end when you finish the last step of the process, but you might need to say something about the implications of the process. Also, ask yourself whether it is worthwhile to summarize what the process did or accomplished.

The following is an example of an essay that narrates a process:

THE TESTING OF HYPOTHESES

In the conduct of an experiment, there are five well-defined steps. The first of these may be called the preparation of the specimen. Accessible material is usually (though not always) brought into the laboratory where it can be properly isolated and got ready: thin sections cut by means of microtomes, slides prepared, control groups selected. Field experimenting requires the choosing of the proper time and place. In geology many hours of exploration are necessary in order to discover exposed strata of the type desired. In the case of inaccessible material, such as astronomical bodies, the time and place for experimental observations will have to be carefully calculated, such as is done before expected eclipses. The British expedition to South Africa led by Eddington immediately after World War I to verify Einstein's prediction that light rays would bend close to the sun's surface is an instance in point.

We have prepared the material to be tested, but what about the apparatus which is to be put to work on the material? The second step involves the preparation of the instrument. There are tasks peculiar to it quite apart from what it may be testing or what may be the results from running a series of experiments. There must be a checking of the equipment before the start of the run. Instruments not in continual operation have to be prepared to operate. Parts must be cleaned, motors tuned. Push buttons, toggle switches, knobs and levers have to be in good working order. If there are tubes, they have to be given time to warm up; if there is a vacuum, several days may be required to pump it up to the required level. Is everything properly oiled and tuned up? Do all meters, indicators and gauges read as they should? Is the apparatus operating properly? Perhaps a dry run is in order here; the instrument can be turned on without the material to be tested just to be sure that all of its parts are in working order. For this purpose a check-list is a good thing to have. Check points can be itemized and used as a reminder for a thorough examination of the apparatus before an experiment is run.

The third step consists in the proper isolation of the experiment. The material to be tested and the apparatus used to do the testing must be removed as a unit from all factors which might constitute interference. Factors ignored or held negligible have the power of cancelling the effectiveness of an experiment. Variables which are not controlled as parts of the experiment must be properly randomized in order to neutralize their interference, for instance by experimenting at different times and if possible also at different places. Randomizing unwanted variables is not an ideal way of eliminating the danger which they constitute, but it is one way of reducing it.

In the case of experiments in the field rather than the laboratory, the third step consists in preparing the site and arranging the conditions under which observations are to take place. When Tinbergen wished to observe the social life of the herring gull under average conditions, he had to prepare his observation site well in advance of the events he had chosen to witness, and he had to spend many hours in concealment in order that the birds might learn to proceed normally in his presence. The behavior of the objects under observation, whether it be the nesting habits of the Kittiwake on the high cliffs of the Farne Islands off the coast of Northumberland, or the occulting periodic of the Cepheid variable stars, requires many hours of vigil and prolonged observations.

The fourth step consists in the running of the experiment. Once the experiment has been begun, the operation of the instrument needs to be watched. Maintenance during the run is important, and in this connection a maintenance check-list may be made up and followed, with oil check-points, dials, levers, etc., listed. There must be no failure of performance which might color the findings. Disturbances arising from inside the apparatus due to fluctuations in its source of power or to increase in noise must be anticipated wherever possible and controlled. Tubes can always blow, circuits go out, ventilation can become clogged, liquid flows can become turbulent, transformers can produce undesirable magnetic fields, moisture can form on cooling coils, mechanical systems can develop oscillations, motors can show vibrations. Such a list would have to include provisions for the aging and wearing of parts as well as for operationally developed maladjustments. These and many similar difficulties can often be anticipated and avoided, though of course not always. If not, they must be met when they occur, and corrections made as the experiment proceeds.

An investigator who is familiar both with the hypothesis he purports to be testing and the construction and operation of the instrument which was designed for the purpose has a better chance of successfully carrying out the experiment than one who is ignorant on some one of these scores. A great deal of fortitude in the face of obstacles and persistence in the face of failures is necessary for the success of some experiments. So much can go wrong, so many little things may have been overlooked in a first run, that the project may be abandoned before it has had a fair chance. Instruments have been discarded for a time, only to be returned to favor at a later date after the occasion for their rejection has been dissipated. Such was the case with Carrel's perfusion pump, which was given up after Carrel's defection to the Vichy French during World War II, only to be taken up again by the biochemists a decade later.

A certain level of sophisticated observation is essential during the running of an experiment. In every experiment there are many conditions to be noticed, as it were, all at once. The various parts of an experiment must be watched and their coordination maintained in order to preserve the continuance of their proper interrelations. If there are relevant factors which may be varied, they must be varied one at a time. Irrelevant factors may be varied to be sure that they are in fact irrelevant. Positive efforts must be continually made to ward against the inadvertent introduction of elements which may constitute serious interference.

An astute experimentalist will be alert to the failure of an experiment. A failure must not be confused with a negative result. An experiment which fails is one which is incapable of giving any result, as for instance when an apparatus breaks down or when there has been found to be sufficient interference to cancel the success of the experiment. Changes in the behavior of materials which are parts of the apparatus when under a high vacuum, immense pressure, enormous speeds, or extremes of heat or cold will have a different meaning from those same changes in the materials which are the subject of experiment. On the other hand, consistency of policy must be maintained: once a factor is judged to be an interference, it must be so judged on all subsequent runs of the same experiment.

The fifth and final step in experimenting calls for the collecting of results. In the case of laboratory experiments automatic recorders, rate meters, counters, scalers and timers must be read carefully, and in the case of field experiments, observations must be recorded. Both should be done promptly, before a lapse of time allows inaccuracies to creep in. The experiments were performed for the sake of the results, and the results will have to be interpreted; but collecting results is often a procedure requiring considerable promptness and great care.

Generally speaking, observation at the experimental level is no longer naive, and the investigator comes to his observations with deliberate preconceptions. He knows what it is that he should expect to see: a movement, a configuration, a pointer-reading, indications as significant in their absence as in their presence. Negative results must be carefully noted; as we have seen, a negative result is not the same as a failure: a properly designed experiment can be successful in yielding either a positive or a negative result. It must not be in science, as Francis Bacon said, that men mark only when they hit and not when they miss. An experiment is the narrowing of the evidence to the relevance of a certain question; however, there is always the possibility of surprise to be kept open.

—James Kern Feibleman

1. Point to Feibleman's identification of the process.
2. Does he identify and provide an overview for each step?
3. How does he make clear the nature of each step?
4. How does he make certain that the reader is oriented along the way?
5. What is the function of the final paragraph? What does it add to the essay?

We include the following selection as much for its advice as for its supplying an example of process. Vonnegut spells out the steps in a process that cannot be separated into sections according to chronology. He explains some of the major points a writer must consider in the process of writing.

HOW TO WRITE WITH STYLE

Newspaper reporters and technical writers are trained to reveal almost nothing about themselves in their writings. This makes them freaks in the world of writers, since almost all of the other ink-stained wretches in that world reveal a lot about themselves to readers. We call these revelations, accidental and intentional, elements of style.

These revelations tell us as readers what sort of person it is with whom we are spending time. Does the writer sound ignorant or informed, stupid or bright, crooked or honest, humorless or playful—? And on and on.

Why should you examine your writing style with the idea of

improving it? Do so as a mark of respect for your readers, whatever you're writing. If you scribble your thoughts any which way, your readers will surely feel that you care nothing about them. They will mark you down as an egomaniac or a chowderhead—or worse, they will stop reading you.

The most damning revelation you can make about yourself is that you do not know what is interesting and what is not. Don't you yourself like or dislike writers mainly for what they choose to show you or make you think about? Did you ever admire an empty-headed writer for his or her mastery of the language? No.

So your own winning style must begin with ideas in your head.

1. FIND A SUBJECT YOU CARE ABOUT

Find a subject you care about and which you in your heart feel others should care about. It is this genuine caring, and not your games with language, which will be the most compelling and seductive element in your style.

I am not urging you to write a novel, by the way—although I would not be sorry if you wrote one, provided you genuinely cared about something. A petition to the mayor about a pothole in front of your house or a love letter to the girl next door will do.

2. DO NOT RAMBLE, THOUGH

I won't ramble on about that.

3. KEEP IT SIMPLE

As for your use of language: Remember that two great masters of language, William Shakespeare and James Joyce, wrote sentences which were almost childlike when their subjects were most profound. "To be or not to be?" asks Shakespeare's Hamlet. The longest word is three letters long. Joyce, when he was frisky, could put together a sentence as intricate and as glittering as a necklace for Cleopatra, but my favorite sentence in his short story "Eveline" is this one: "She was tired." At that point in the story, no other words could break the heart of a reader as those three words do.

Simplicity of language is not only reputable, but perhaps even sacred. The *Bible* opens with a sentence well within the writing skills of a lively fourteen-year-old: "In the beginning God created the heaven and the earth."

4. HAVE THE GUTS TO CUT

It may be that you, too, are capable of making necklaces for Cleopatra, so to speak. But your eloquence should be the servant of the ideas in your head. Your rule might be this: If a sentence, no matter how excellent, does not illuminate your subject in some new and useful way, scratch it out.

5. SOUND LIKE YOURSELF

The writing style which is most natural for you is bound to echo the speech you heard when a child. English was the novelist Joseph Conrad's third language, and much that seems piquant in his use of English was no doubt colored by his first language, which was Polish. And lucky indeed is the writer who has grown up in Ireland, for the English spoken there is so amusing and musical. I myself grew up in Indianapolis, where common speech sounds like a band saw cutting galvanized tin, and employs a vocabulary as unornamental as a monkey wrench.

In some of the more remote hollows of Appalachia, children still grow up hearing songs and locutions of Elizabethan times. Yes, and many Americans grow up hearing a language other than English, or an English dialect a majority of Americans cannot understand.

All of these varieties of speech are beautiful, just as the varieties of butterflies are beautiful. No matter what your first language, you should treasure it all your life. If it happens not to be standard English, and if it shows itself when you write standard English, the result is usually delightful, like a very pretty girl with one eye that is green and one that is blue.

I myself find that I trust my own writing most, and others seem to trust it most, too, when I sound most like a person from Indianapolis, which is what I am. What alternatives do I have? The one most vehemently recommended by teachers has no doubt been pressed on you, as well: to write like cultivated Englishmen of a century or more ago.

6. SAY WHAT YOU MEAN TO SAY

I used to be exasperated by such teachers, but am no more. I understand now that all those antique essays and stories with which I was to compare my own work were not magnificent for their datedness or foreignness, but for saying precisely what their authors meant them to say. My teachers wished me to write accurately, always selecting the most effective words, and relating the words to one another unambiguously, rigidly, like parts of a machine. The teachers did not want to turn me into an Englishman after all. They hoped that I would become understandable—and therefore understood. And there went my dream of doing with words what Pablo Picasso did with paint or what any number of jazz idols did with music. If I broke all the rules of punctuation, had words mean whatever I wanted them to mean, and strung them together higgledy-piggledy, I would simply not be understood. So you, too, had better avoid Picasso-style or jazz-style writing, if you have something worth saying and wish to be understood.

Readers want our pages to look very much like pages they have seen before. Why? This is because they themselves have a tough job to do, and they need all the help they can get from us.

7. PITY THE READERS

They have to identify thousands of little marks on paper, and make sense of them immediately. They have to *read,* an art so difficult that most people don't really master it even after having studied it all through grade school and high school—twelve long years.

So this discussion must finally acknowledge that our stylistic options as writers are neither numerous nor glamorous, since our readers are bound to be such imperfect artists. Our audience requires us to be sympathetic and patient teachers, ever willing to simplify and clarify—whereas we would rather soar high above the crowd, singing like nightingales.

That is the bad news. The good news is that we Americans are governed under a unique Constitution, which allows us to write whatever we please without fear of punishment. So the most meaningful aspect of our styles, which is what we choose to write about, is utterly unlimited.

8. FOR REALLY DETAILED ADVICE

For a discussion of literary style in a narrower sense, in a more technical sense, I commend to your attention *The Elements of Style*, by William Strunk, Jr., and E. B. White (Macmillan, 1979). E. B. White is, of course, one of the most admirable literary stylists this country has so far produced.

You should realize, too, that no one would care how well or badly Mr. White expressed himself, if he did not have perfectly enchanting things to say.

—Kurt Vonnegut

EXERCISES

1. Because so many students have complained that the process of registering for classes is so confusing on your campus, the student government has appointed a committee to write a brief, clear narrative telling students how the process of registration occurs. The narrative will appear in a brochure going to all new students. Using the design for processes, write the section on registration for the brochure.

2. Everyone knows how to do at least one thing well, be it spinning a frisbee or trimming hedges. Explain a process you do well to a reader who has never tried it.

3. At one time or another, most people have thought about going to small claims court because they think someone has taken advantage of them. But most people do not know how to go about filing a claim and getting it into court. Your student government has decided that students should know how to use the small claims court and has asked you to prepare a handout that can be given to students who come to the offices with complaints about landlords or local merchants. Prepare a handout telling students how to use the small claims court.

EXPLAINING CONCEPTS

A large persimmon tree in a neighbor's yard always leads those unfamiliar with persimmons to ask about them. What do they look like? What do they taste like? How often is the work "like" central to questions and explanations of something not understood? Persimmons look *like* large tomatoes, although (another word for *unlike*) they are more orange in color. A ripe persimmon has the consistency of jelly (i.e., is *like* jelly).

Explaining concepts requires seeing relationships. We learn by relating what we don't know to what we do know and then by seeing the differences between the known and the unknown. (Persimmons look like large tomatoes—similarity—although they are more orange in color—difference.) Most genuine learning comes through the process of comparing and distinguishing. Memorizing facts or theorems only slightly enhances our understanding of something. To understand and appreciate the implications of a fact or theorem, we must *react* to it. We compare the new with the known. We test new knowledge against the yardstick of accepted categories. This skeptical, probing comparative tendency of the mind integrates new knowledge and experience into our view of life and the world. The process of seeing relationships is what most people mean by the word *thinking*. Seeing relationships underlies most of science and all of literature. And it provides the basic designs for explaining concepts, ideas, and theories.

A design for explaining concepts (called *exposition* in traditional rhetorical theory) is needed when a writer wants to consider something:

1. Side by side with something else (persimmons and tomatoes).
2. As the result of something else (the effect of fertilizer on the size of persimmons).
3. As part of a system (the persimmon as a member of the ebony family of trees).

As with description and narration, a writer rarely cares about simply seeing two things side by side, seeing one thing as the result of another, or seeing something as part of a system. A purpose comes first, and the writer chooses a design to achieve the purpose. A writer's purpose might be to determine which turbine will best suit a particular power plant. The writer's final report might compare one kind of turbine with three others, explain how each turbine will affect the system for which it is designed, and explain how the turbine will fit into the system. In addition the writer might describe the turbine and parts of the system, tell how a turbine works, and then narrate the history of the project, consequently using all the flexible designs we have looked at so far. As with the other flexible designs, the designs for explaining concepts can be applied whenever you see that your purpose is to explain. Because concepts involve the qualities things have, the concepts you explain can run from complex economic theories, such as communism, to stuff of ordinary experience, such as persimmons.

Comparison

Writers put concepts side by side for two purposes: to clarify one concept by setting it against something better understood and to understand or evaluate two or more concepts by systematically considering their likenesses and differences. The first process is *analogy;* the second is *comparison and contrast.*

Analogy. Analogies help a reader to understand a concept. Seldom longer than a paragraph, analogies function like examples to help convey the writer's immediate point. While an example is a specific instance of a concept, an analogy searches for a well-known concept resembling a lesser known concept to help the reader understand the unknown through the known.

> An *example:* Effective firefighting occurred *when crews quickly controlled the September fire on Bishop's Peak.*

> An *analogy:* Effective firefighting is *like herding sheep with trained dogs.*

Notice that both examples need further explanation: we want the details of the firefighting to understand why the Bishop's Peak fire is a good example of firefighting, and we want to know in what ways firefighting resembles herding sheep with trained dogs. Examples need enough detail to illustrate the writer's point, and analogies need several points of comparison so that the reader can be led from the known to the unknown.

Let us consider an example of *analogy:*

It is quite easy for an American to see that our decimal system of coinage is better than the traditional (but soon to be

changed) British system of pounds, shillings, and pence (not to mention half-crowns and guineas), because it is simpler in principle and very much more convenient to handle. But it is not nearly so easy for us to see that the metric system of weights and measures has exactly the same advantage over our curious conglomeration of ounces and pounds, inches, feet, yards, and miles, pints, quarts, and gallons, and so forth. We may admit the advantage in theory, but we are likely to have a deep-seated feeling that our units are somehow real, and the metrical ones merely clever tricks. It is very hard indeed for most of us to think of a hundred meters as simply a hundred meters, or as a tenth of a kilometer. We feel that it is really a hundred and nine-point-something yards, and wonder why the silly foreigners couldn't at least have made it come out an even hundred and ten. And of course the kilometer is too short to be a serious way of measuring long distances. How can anybody be satisfied with anything that isn't quite five-eighths of a mile?

In a very similar way most of us have a strong feeling that the sort of grammar to which we were exposed when young is somehow real, and that any different analysis of our language is tampering with the truth. But there is no more reason to believe that all words fall naturally into eight parts of speech than there is to think that silver comes naturally in either dollars or shillings, or butter in pounds or kilograms. We may have been taught that the sacred eight were permanent realities, no more open to question than the Ten Commandments or the multiplication table. Yet, since the second English grammar was written, there has never been a time when "the authorities" agreed on what or how many the parts were (every number from zero to ten has been advocated), to say nothing of what words belonged in each part; and just now the disagreement is particularly acute.

—L. M. Meyers, *The Roots of Modern English*

Meyers notes likenesses between two things not normally considered in relationship to each other. By juxtaposing the metric system of measurement with the parts of speech in English, he clarifies a concept (how tenaciously we cling to our comfortable but inaccurate ways of arranging experience).

Consider one more example of *analogy,* this time relying on narrative and on point-by-point development of the analogy's meaning:

And he began again to teach by the sea side: and there was gathered unto him a great multitude, so that he entered into a ship, and sat in the sea; and the whole multitude was by the sea on the land. And he taught them many things by parables, and said unto them in his doctrine, "Hearken; Behold, there went out a sower to sow: and it came to pass, as he sowed, some fell by the way side, and the fowls of the air came and devoured it up. And some fell on stony ground, where it had not much earth; and immediately it sprang up, because it had no depth of earth: but when the sun was up, it was scorched; and because it had no root, it withered away. And some fell among thorns, and the thorns grew up, and choked it, and it yielded no fruit. And others fell on good ground, and did yield fruit that sprang up and increased; and brought forth, some thirty, and some sixty, and some an hundred." And he said unto them, "He that hath ears to hear, let him hear."

And when he was alone, they that were about him with the twelve asked of him the parable. And he said unto them, "Unto you it is given to know the mystery of the kingdom of God: but unto them that are without, all these things are done in parables: that seeing they may see, and not perceive; and hearing they may hear, and not understand; lest at any time they should be converted, and their sins should be forgiven them." And he said unto them, "Know ye not this parable? and how then will ye know all parables? The sower soweth the word. And these are they by the way side, where the word is sown; but when they have heard, Satan cometh immediately, and taketh away the word that was sown in their hearts. And these are they likewise which are sown on stony ground; who, when they have heard the word, immediately receive it with gladness; and have no root in themselves, and so endure but for a time: afterward, when affliction or persecution ariseth for the word's sake, immediately they are offended. And these are they that are sown among thorns; such as hear the word, and the cares of this world, and the deceitfulness of riches, and the lusts of other things entering in, choke the word, and it becometh unfruitful. And these are they which are sown on good ground;

such as hear the word, and receive it, and bring forth fruit, some thirty-fold, some sixty, and some an hundred.''
—Mark, 4:1–20

Mark compares a seed to the word of God, suggesting that God's word will only be received, nurtured, and grown to fruition in those men who are ready for it. By its references to ordinary experience, the analogy helps a reader to understand the concept of how God's word affects people.

A Design for Analogy

1. *Preparation.* The reader needs to know right away that you are using an analogy to explain a concept (unless your analogy leads into a subject as does the analogy in Meyers's introduction to grammar). Often it takes only a word or two to make certain your reader knows you are using an analogy. The word "like," for example, will tip off your reader.

2. *Expansion.* An analogy is an extended comparison. Because the purpose of an analogy is to clarify, concentrate on the ways in which the two concepts resemble each other. Since you need not prove that the two concepts are actually alike, analogies need not be precise. But the comparison should lead your reader to a clearer understanding of the concept you wish to explain.

A word of warning: analogies can take on a life of their own and

---

ANALOGY

Preparation:
  Indicate that you are using an analogy to make a point.
Expansion:
  Develop the similarities one by one.
  Avoid elaborate comparisons.
Closure:
  Make your point and return to the discourse.

become so elaborate that after awhile they lead a reader away from understanding. Stick to the key points of the analogy, and get back to the thread of the discourse as quickly as possible.

3. *Closure.* Most analogies work like jokes: you understand the meaning at the end. The topic and direction of both jokes and analogies are clear at the beginning, but the writer gradually adds information. By the end, the precise meaning becomes clear. Once the point of your analogy has been made, go directly back to the larger discourse that your analogy has helped to develop.

Here is an example of an analogy used to begin an editorial in a newspaper:

> Coyotes are superb creatures. It is exhilarating to spot them silently roaming in the evening dusk, in the grassy hills. But it's disturbing to have to yield them the right of way when biking to work. We delude ourselves when we think that if we feed them, we will tame them. Instead, they merely come to depend on the food. Eliminate it, and they will not go away nor try to ingratiate themselves by wagging their tails. They'll go after your cats, dogs, children.
>
> Humans are no different. The American emergency plan to seize Saudi Arabian oil fields in the event of an oil embargo made waves a few years ago. The waves are gone, but not the plans. Americans have come to consider Arab oil something they are entitled to, simply because they are badly dependent on it. Have someone turn off the pipeline, and the reaction is to send in the Marines to secure "our" oil supply, although even a successful invasion would destroy the source. We don't try to satisfy ourselves with domestic supplies and conservation. Nor do we try to ingratiate ourselves with the oil suppliers. Selling oil does not give the Saudis influence over the United States. Money, yes—in inflationary dollars weakened by excessive oil purchases. Power, no—especially not the power to threaten with an oil embargo. The Saudis have been feeding the coyotes too much for too long, and it is dangerous for both sides.
>
> Soviet rulers are no different. Make them dependent on American grain, and they'll come to consider it their due. American influence will actually decrease. The more they depend on this grain, the less Washington can risk agitating them with embargo threats. If the alternative were widespread starvation in the Soviet Union, they would be sorely tempted to seize

"their" corn fields, or whatever is left of them after a "rapid deployment" of nuclear force. Meanwhile, grain trade helps the United States make money, or whatever one calls the IOUs tendered by a deeply indebted empire. Midwestern votes are all that one can buy with such funny money.

—Rein Taagepera, "Why Are We Feeding The Ravenous Russians?"

1. What is the purpose of the second paragraph? Why doesn't the writer go directly from the analogy of paragraph 1 to the point of paragraph 3?
2. Why does the writer develop each analogy separately? Why doesn't he explain how each point of the first two analogies applies to the points of paragraphs 2 and 3?

Here is an example of an analogy used as the basis of an essay:

RESPECT FOR A NEW HOME, A NEW MARRIAGE

Slowly, it is becoming our house. With each new coat of paint, each box unpacked, each tile set into place, we begin to feel our presence in its past.

The house is old, and built of solid mid-19th-Century stock. It doesn't give way to its latest inhabitants. Nor do we lay claim as if it were virgin territory and we were land-rushing pioneers.

We treat the house, the house that is slowly becoming ours, with some respect. We, after all, have moved into it. It may be our new house, but we are its newcomers.

From the beginning, we paid homage to its prior life. This is what we chose—the old brick, the fireplaces, the woods that become warm and worn with time. Newcomers, we didn't create this building, but we accept its patches and imperfections.

At the same time, we do not regard ourselves as curators in a museum. This is not Sturbridge Village. Yes, other families have settled here, other lives have been played out here. But now it is our time. We renovate, renew this structure, make changes. Slowly it is becoming ours.

I stand in the middle of the living room, empty except for a plant and a piano, and think of how different this is from moving into a brand-new house. Here we seek some balance between its history and our future.

It is like this, I think, with second marriages, or perhaps just mid-life marriages. In a few days, before the last box is unpacked, the last faucet is in working order, we will be married. It has not been what our families call a whirlwind courtship. We are among the lucky people who were friends first and didn't lose the friendship in love.

Our first marriages, like most, followed a predictable outline. Each of us married, bore children, bought houses. This time, as if to break the jinx, we have begun the reel in reverse.

Young people, first-timers if you will, take on marriage as if it were a plot of land. With luck, they build something new and welcoming. With luck, they always feel at home with each other.

But second-timers are natural renovators. We know the structure of marriage enough to be wary of the ways in which the foundation weakens. We know it enough to seek comfort again in its shelter and support. More than that, we have learned something about balancing a respect for one another's past with a need to create something that will be ours.

Like many second-timers, we come to this marriage with two sets of china and children. Like most people in mid-life, we come equally well-equipped with experiences. Over decades, all of us acquire friendships, careers, habits, ideas, ideals, and the stuff that sticks together and becomes the self.

Renovators, re-marriers, learn to tip a hat to that self, the life that we move into, the one that we have chosen. We are more hesitant about knocking down supporting walls, relationships, egos. We are more conscious of the energy that went into their creation.

Newcomers to a second marriage, we know the cracks, the flaws in each other's lives. We take note of all the vulnerable places where partial repairs have been made of the past damage.

Yet we also acknowledge a desire, a right, to make changes, to build something out of these pasts that we can live with comfortably. We make careful plans, respectful renovations, changes.

This home that I am standing in is still in process. There is a box of table linen somewhere. A sink is missing between the

manufacturer and the plumber. But slowly this is becoming our
house. Slowly, too, this will become our marriage.

—Ellen Goodman

1. At what point do you realize that Goodman is constructing
an analogy?
2. Point to each element of the analogy.
3. Why does Goodman focus the first six paragraphs on the
house rather than move quickly to the subject of second
marriages?
4. What is the point of her analogy?

EXERCISES

1. In a letter to a friend, use an analogy to explain what it is
like to be a freshman.
2. For your obituary, find an analogy to explain your proudest moment.
3. For your autobiography, find an analogy to explain the
most intense emotion you have felt during your life.
4. For a textbook you are working on, find an analogy to
explain a scientific concept to junior high school students.

Comparison and contrast. If you are in the market for a new car,
you might rush down to the nearest Ford agency and take whatever
strikes your fancy. Most people, though, shop less impulsively, especially for expensive items. Shopping involves comparing items: What
is the price of each? What features? How well made? How
dependable?

Writers use the designs for *comparison and contrast* for two reasons: to evaluate or to understand. Any time you want to choose one
thing over others logically (as opposed to impulsively), you set up
criteria, compare the products in each category of your criteria, and
arrive at an overall judgment. In buying a car, you might decide that
you will limit yourself to compact sedans costing less than $7,000. At
that point you can set up your criteria, which might include reliability, comfort, handling, power, and nearness of a dealership. After
defining for yourself what you seek in each category, you can begin
the process of comparison. In other situations, you might want to

compare two things simply to understand both better. For example, you might want to compare the batting rules in the American League with those in the National League. Or you might want to compare the subway systems of New York and London.

Let us look at one comparison used to evaluate and one used to understand:

French fries aren't small potatoes in the fast-food business. To *McDonald's,* for instance, the spuds are reportedly worth more than $1-billion a year, or almost 20 percent of yearly revenue. The company has gone so far as to patent its french-frying methods. Just how tasty are those centerpieces of the kwik-food menu? CU decided to find out.

We sent our taste experts to six big chains: *Arby's, Arthur Treacher's, Burger King, McDonald's, Roy Rogers,* and *Wendy's* all in the New York City area. Our experts judged the fries on the spot in each restaurant, and then again as a take-out order, 15 minutes after receiving them. They repeated the procedure in a second restaurant of each chain.

McDonald's fixation on the potato would seem to pay off; our tasters rated its shoestring potatoes very good, the highest rating any fast-food fries received. The fries were consistently hot, crisp, and golden brown, with tender insides, a distinct potato taste, and a light flavoring of oil. While they didn't match CU's homemade spuds, they were as good as the best of the frozen potatoes we tested. They did, however, suffer in takeout orders; as they cooled, they became soggy and less flavorful. They also tended to arrive with too much salt, but they can be ordered salt-free or with "light" salt.

Consistency was not a hallmark at *Arthur Treacher's.* One store provided its potatoes in a chubby steak cut, with the skins left on; those were touted as "natural potatoes." The second styled its potatoes "chips" and supplied them in a steak cut with lengthwise crinkles. In both shapes, the fries were judged good, with a slight starchy aftertaste; the chips also had a slightly chewy texture.

Our tasters judged *Roy Rogers* fries good because they didn't consistently offer the crisp-outside/tender-inside combination and because they tended to be a shade greasy. One *Roy Rogers* restaurant didn't presalt its fries; the other oversalted its fries a bit.

Wendy's potatoes came in a regular cut, decently golden and crisp/tender from one store, slightly starchy and cardboardy from the other. They too were judged good. *Burger King's* shoestring fries, judged fair to good, tended to be greasy and left a slight starchy aftertaste. The *Arby's* shoestring fries proved the most variable, ranging in one store from underdone to dark and hard, but in both stores always smacking excessively of grease. Overall, they were only fair.

One final note on the fast fries: In both *Wendy's* and *Burger King,* it didn't pay to buy the large size, which cost more per ounce than their small package of fries. And there was no discount for quantity at *McDonald's*—the small and large orders cost the same per ounce of fries.

—Consumer Reports

Let me outline as briefly as I can what seem to me the characteristics of these opposite kinds of mind [exploiter and nurturer, terms suggesting not only a division "between persons" but also "within persons"]. I conceive a strip-miner to be a model exploiter, and as a model nurturer I take the old-fashioned idea or ideal of a farmer. The exploiter is a specialist, an expert; the nurturer is not. The standard of the exploiter is efficiency; the standard of the nurturer is care. The exploiter's goal is money, profit; the nurturer's goal is health—his land's health, his own, his family's, his community's, his country's. Whereas the exploiter asks of a piece of land only how much and how quickly it can be made to produce, the nurturer asks a question that is much more complex and difficult: What is its carrying capacity? (That is: How much can be taken from it without diminishing it? What can it produce *dependably* for an indefinite time?) The exploiter wishes to earn as much as possible by as little work as possible; the nurturer expects, certainly, to have a decent living from his work, but his characteristic wish is to work *as well* as possible. The competence of the exploiter is in organization; that of the nurturer is in order— a human order, that is, that accommodates itself both to other order and to mystery. The exploiter typically serves an institution or organization; the nurturer serves land, household, community, place. The exploiter thinks in terms of numbers, quantities, "hard facts"; the nurturer in terms of character, condition, quality, kind.

—Wendell Berry, *The Unsettling of America*

To compare for evaluation and to compare for understanding sound like quite different purposes, but a writer sets about doing each in the same way. The first step is to be certain that you have established a *basis* for comparison. Have you heard that apples and oranges cannot be compared? Nonsense. How about comparing their seasonal cycles? Their sugars? Their nutritional value? The core of a comparison is not the objects being compared, but what about them you choose to compare. Clearly you cannot compare the seasonal cycles of oranges with the nutritional value of apples. No basis exists for the comparison. But you can compare their nutritional value. When comparing, first establish a precise basis for comparison. In comparing two characters in a novel, for example, you might choose to compare the ways in which they gain self-awareness. In comparing two bacteria, you might compare the way they absorb stains.

Let us look at a complete design for *comparison and contrast*.

A Design for Comparison and Contrast

1. *Preparation.* Establish a clear basis of comparison, and be certain that the reader understands it. Next, provide any background that will help to orient the reader. If it would be useful, tell the reader the categories you will use for the comparison.

2. *Expansion.* Because comparison focuses equally on two or more things, any design for expansion must give equal and parallel attention to each thing. Here are two forms of organization for comparing two things. If you wish to compare more than two, simply add on. The example compares backpacks (the topic) for extended summer trips on mountain trails (the basis for comparison). The first design is organized by topics; the second design treats each part of the subject independently, addressing each topic under each subject.

DESIGN 1: TOPICS

I. Frame Design
  A. Shape
    1. Pack 1
    2. Pack 2
  B. Suspension
    1. Shoulder
      a. Pack 1
      b. Pack 2

DESIGN 2: SUBJECT

I. Pack 1
  A. Frame Design
    1. Shape
    2. Suspension
      a. Shoulder
      b. Waist

2. Waist
  a. Pack 1
  b. Pack 2
II. Pack Design
  A. Main Compartment
    1. Capacity
      a. Pack 1
      b. Pack 2
    2. Arrangement
      a. Pack 1
      b. Pack 2
  B. Pockets
    1. Capacity
      a. Pack 1
      b. Pack 2
    2. Arrangement
      a. Pack 1
      b. Pack 2
  C. Additional Features
    1. Crampon Arrangements
      a. Pack 1
      b. Pack 2
    2. Ice-axe Arrangement
      a. Pack 1
      b. Pack 2
III. Materials
  A. Frame
    1. Pack 1
    2. Pack 2
  B. Pack
    1. Pack 1
    2. Pack 2

B. Pack Design
  1. Main Compartment
    a. Capacity
    b. Arrangement
  2. Pockets
    a. Capacity
    b. Arrangement
  3. Additional Features
    a. Crampon Arrangements
    b. Ice-axe Arrangements
C. Materials
  1. Frame
  2. Pack
II. Pack 2
  A. Frame Design
    1. Shape
    2. Suspension
      a. Shoulder
      b. Waist
  B. Pack Design
    1. Main Compartment
      a. Capacity
      b. Arrangement
    2. Pockets
      a. Capacity
      b. Arrangement
    3. Additional Features
      a. Crampon Arrangements
      b. Ice-axe Arrangements
  C. Materials
    1. Frame
    2. Pack

Both designs offer advantages. If your comparison is to be short, design 2 might work best. Focus on the first item and then systematically look at each category for comparison. Then do the same thing with the next item. But don't be misled by the apparent simplicity of this design. Both you and your reader can easily get lost in it, especially if your comparison runs more than a page. Writers often lose their sense of purpose when attempting this design, forgetting to concentrate on comparison and instead simply describing. Unless you have a tight outline, like the one just presented, you also might find yourself drifting into other categories. As a rule of thumb, use design 2 only when your comparison will run less than a page (usually one paragraph for each item).

Design 1 will probably be the most useful for structuring complex comparisons. It keeps the items being compared close together so that the reader (as well as the writer) can see the relationship between the two. It also prevents you from forgetting to discuss in one section something that you mention in another.

Which form of organization is used in the example from *Consumer Reports* and the one by Wendell Berry?

3. *Closure.* Comparisons often end with some sort of summary statement. If your purpose is to *evaluate,* you will need to pull together the various strengths and weaknesses of each item, sorting

---

COMPARISON AND CONTRAST

Preparation:

   Establish a clear basis of comparison.

   Provide any background information that will help to orient the reader.

   If useful, name the categories you will use.

Expansion:

   Select one of the two standard forms of organization: (1) a point-by-point comparison or (2) a survey of all points for each item being compared.

   Use the categories to compare things systematically.

Closure:

   If you use comparison for evaluation, summarize strengths and weaknesses, and decide which item is better.

   If you use comparison for understanding, summarize similarities and differences, and indicate their significance.

through them and coming to some conclusion about which seems better in terms of your basis of comparison. If your purpose is to *understand,* you might want to summarize the main similarities and differences and then point to their significance.

The following is an example of comparison from Mark Twain's *Life on the Mississippi:*

TWO VIEWS OF THE MISSISSIPPI

The face of the water, in time, became a wonderful book—a book that was a dead language to the uneducated passenger, but which told its mind to me without reserve, delivering its most cherished secrets as clearly as if it uttered them with a voice. And it was not a book to be read once and thrown aside, for it had a new story to tell every day. Throughout the long twelve hundred miles there was never a page that was void of interest, never one that you could leave unread without loss, never one that you would want to skip, thinking you could find higher enjoyment in some other thing. There never was so wonderful a book written by man; never one whose interest was so absorbing, so unflagging, so sparklingly renewed with every reperusal. The passenger who could not read it was charmed with a peculiar sort of faint dimple on its surface (on the rare occasions when he did not overlook it altogether); but to the pilot that was an *italicized* passage; indeed, it was more than that, it was a legend of the largest capitals, with a string of shouting exclamation points at the end of it; for it meant that a wreck or a rock was buried there that could tear the life out of the strongest vessel that ever floated. It is the faintest and simplest expression that water ever makes, and the most hideous to a pilot's eye. In truth, the passenger who could not read this book saw nothing but all manner of pretty pictures in it, painted by the sun and shaded by the clouds, whereas to the trained eye these were not pictures at all, but the grimmest and most dead-earnest of reading matter.

Now when I had mastered the language of this water and had come to know every trifling feature that bordered the great river as familiarly as I knew the letters of the alphabet, I had made a valuable acquisition. But I had lost something, too. I had lost something which could never be restored to me while I lived. All the grace, the beauty, the poetry had gone out of the majestic river! I still keep in mind a certain wonderful sunset which I witnessed when steamboating was new to me. A broad expanse of the river was turned to blood; in the middle distance the red hue brightened into gold, through which a solitary log came floating, black and conspicuous; in one place a long, slanting mark lay sparkling upon the water; in another the surface was broken by boiling, tumbling rings, that were as many-tinted as an opal; where the ruddy flush was faintest, was a smooth spot that was covered with graceful circles and radiating lines, ever so delicately traced; the shore on our left was densely wooded, and the somber shadow that fell from this forest was broken in one place by a long, ruffled trail that shone like silver; and high above the forest wall a clean-stemmed dead tree waved a single leafy bough that glowed like a flame in the unobstructed splendor that was flowing from the sun. There were graceful curves, reflected images, woody heights, soft distances; and over the whole scene, far and near, the dissolving lights drifted steadily, enriching it, every passing moment, with new marvels of coloring.

I stood like one bewitched. I drank it in, in a speechless rapture. The world was new to me, and I had never seen anything like this at home. But as I have said, a day came when I began to cease from noting the glories and the charms which the moon and the sun and the twilight wrought upon the river's face; another day came when I ceased altogether to note them. Then, if that sunset scene had been repeated, I should have looked upon it without rapture, and should have commented upon it, inwardly, after this fashion: This sun means that we are going to have wind tomorrow; that floating log means that the river is rising, small thanks to it; that slanting mark on the water refers to a bluff reef which is going to kill somebody's steamboat one of these nights, if it keeps on stretching out like that; those tumbling "boils" show a dissolving bar and a changing channel there; the lines and circles in the slick water over yonder are a warning that that troublesome place is shoaling up dangerously; that silver streak in the shadow of the forest is the "break" from a new snag, and he has located himself in the very best place he could have found to fish for steamboats; that tall dead tree, with a single living branch, is not going to last long, and then how is a body ever going to get through this blind place at night without the friendly old landmark?

No, the romance and the beauty were all gone from the river. All the value any feature of it had for me now was the amount of usefulness it could furnish toward compassing the safe piloting of a steamboat. Since those days, I have pitied doctors from my heart. What does the lovely flush in a beauty's cheek mean to a doctor but a "break" that ripples above some deadly disease? Are not all her visible charms sown thick with what are to him the signs and symbols of hidden decay? Does he ever see her beauty at all, or doesn't he simply view her professionally, and comment upon her unwholesome condition all to himself? And doesn't he sometimes wonder whether he has gained most or lost most by learning his trade?

—Mark Twain

1. How does Twain establish a basis for his comparison?
2. What points does Twain compare? What are the two views of the Mississippi?
3. Why does Twain refer to a book? Is this a comparison? List the points of similarity and then explain what Twain tries to reveal.
4. Does Twain use comparison to evaluate or to clarify? What is evaluated or clarified?
5. Is Twain an observer or a participant? A novice or an expert? How does he use these categories in his comparison?

EXERCISES

1. For a newspaper's feature article on gifts for high school graduates, you have been assigned to do a section on watches. Since both digital and analog watches are popular, you have decided to compare the two types. Compare and contrast the two kinds of watches.
2. Everyone has some purchase he or she would like to make if only the money were available. Narrow your choice of options for that purchase to two products and write them down on a piece of paper. For example, you might select two kinds of running shoes or two kinds of single-lens reflex cameras. Exchange your selections with someone in your class, and prepare a report for the other person com-

paring the two products the other person is interested in purchasing.

3. For a brochure being distributed to all new students on your campus, compare three different dormitory complexes.

4. For your autobiography, compare what you are like publicly with what you are like privately.

5. For a popular magazine, write an article comparing two methods of doing something (cooking salmon, splitting wood, planting roses, skinning a cat).

Classification

People like to put things into categories. We place other human beings into groups based on sex, or race, or religion. We distinguish between wild and tame animals. We separate wines into reds, whites, and rosés. Categories for classification depend upon a single, shared characteristic that must be applied consistently. Biologists, for example, classify animals into those with backbones and those without (vertebrates and invertebrates). Only the presence or absence of a backbone decides an animal's classification at this level. Such either-or thinking accounts for much of the classifying people do: we divide our world into smokers and nonsmokers, drivers and nondrivers, degree-holders and nondegree-holders, married people and unmarried people.

While either-or categories show up often in life, writers usually try to find three or more categories. Whatever appears in a "non" category might have little coherence besides being "non," and it might form such a large category that no useful division of the subject takes place.For example, how much sense would it make to write about cowboys and noncowboys? Wrestlers and nonwrestlers? Instead, look for a single unit calling for several divisions (common professions in ranching areas or sports involving body contact). Since all things share traits with other things, anything and everything can be put into sensible groupings.

Each classification comes from the human mind's recognition of relationships. Classifications are not inherently true but, rather, are mental inventions that can be formed and reformed endlessly. How many ways, for example, can you classify students? (Here is a list to get you started: by academic achievement, by athletic participation, by residence, by age, by political sentiments.) At the same time, the categories invented by the human mind have real value. Classification helps us to understand our environment by recognizing the relationships between things.

Let us look, for example, at how one person uses classification to make sense of the power assembly of a motorcycle:

> **The power assembly may be divided into the engine and the power-delivery system. The engine will be taken up first.**
>
> **The engine consists of a housing containing a power train, a fuel-air system, an ignition system, a feedback system and a lubricating system.**
>
> **The power train consists of cylinders, pistons, connecting rods, a crankshaft and a flywheel.**
>
> **The fuel-air system components, which are part of the engine, consist of a gas tank and filter, an air cleaner, a carburetor, valves and exhaust pipes.**
>
> **The ignition system consists of an alternator, a rectifier, a battery, a high-voltage coil and spark plugs.**
>
> **The feedback system consists of a cam chain, a camshaft, tappets and a distributor.**
>
> **The lubrication system consists of an oil pump and channels throughout the housing for distribution of the oil.**
>
> **The power-delivery system accompanying the engine consists of a clutch, a transmission and a chain.**
>
> **The supporting assembly accompanying the power assembly consists of a frame, including foot pegs, seat and fenders; a steering assembly; front and rear shock absorbers; wheels; control levers and cables; lights and horn; and speed and mileage indicators.**
>
> **—Robert Pirsig, *Zen and the Art of Motorcycle Maintenance***

Pirsig divides the power assembly into two parts, turns to the first part (the engine), lists its parts, and then details the segments of each component. He then follows the same procedure for pieces of the power assembly. From his short discussion, the reader can quickly outline the divisions and subdivisions of the power assembly of a motorcycle. Even though Pirsig begins with two categories (engine and power-delivery system), neither of those categories is a "non" category. Most of the subdivisions contain multiple categories, but not so many that a reader will be confused.

A Design for Classification

1. *Preparation.* Begin by identifying what you intend to classify. A familiar topic will need only naming (apples, refrigerators), but a lesser known topic (crampons or motorcycle fairings) invites definition or explanation.

Next, establish a basis for classification. As in comparison, *classification* requires establishing clear grounds for putting things in groups. If you were to classify campus buildings, you would not want to begin with color and shift to style. Your purpose will determine the basis of your classification. A teacher might assign you to classify the various styles of architecture found on campus, or a consulting firm might ask you to classify buildings according to their state of repair to prepare a schedule for renovation.

2. *Expansion.* Name each category stemming from your basis of classification. If you wish to describe wind-powered boats (a classification assuming other sources of power for boats, such as motor power and human power), you will need to label your categories. You might decide that the best way to classify wind-powered boats is by hull design. Your classifications might be single-hulled boats, double-hulled boats, and triple-hulled boats. You might need to find further degrees of subclassification, such as dividing double-hulled boats into catamarans and outriggers.

Explain each classification and subclassification. The name will orient your reader, but the characteristics of the classification deserve explanation. What characterizes an outrigger? How can you distinguish between an outrigger and a catamaran? Your *expansion* section should define clearly the traits making up each category.

Classifications should be explained in the most obvious order. It would not make sense to begin with double-hulled boats, go to single-hulled, and end with triple-hulled. Sometimes the basis for the order is physical (as with the numbers of hulls), and sometimes the basis for the order lies in complexity or importance.

3. *Closure.* Be certain that your reader has grasped the purpose or significance of your classification. Usually your classification will be part of a larger discourse. If so, make clear how the classification contributes to the overall purpose. If, on the other hand, your classification stands alone (as in a biology text's explanation of how to classify mollusks), your focus in closure will probably be on the significance of classifying things in the way you have chosen.

CLASSIFICATION

Preparation:
 Identify what you intend to classify.
 Point out your basis for classification.

Expansion:
 Name each category stemming from your basis of classification.
 Explain each classification and subclassification in the most obvious order.

Closure:
 Be certain that your reader grasps the purpose and significance of your classification.

Here is an example of a brief use of classification from a novel:

Jenny made her own divisions among the non-accidents that happened to the soldiers; she came up with her own categories for them.

1. There were the men who'd been burned; for the most part, they'd been burned on board ship (the most complicated cases came from Chelsea Naval Hospital), but they'd also been burned in airplanes and on the ground. Jenny called them the Externals.

2. There were the men who'd been shot or damaged in bad places; internally, they were in trouble, and Jenny called them the Vital Organs.

3. There were the men whose injuries seemed almost mystical, to Jenny; they were men who weren't "there" anymore, whose heads or spines had been tampered with. Sometimes they were paralyzed, sometimes they were merely vague. Jenny called them the Absentees. Occasionally, one of the Absentees had External or Vital Organ damage as well; all the hospital had a name for them.

4. They were Goners.

—John Irving, *The World According to Garp*

1. What does Irving have his character (Jenny) classify?
2. In what way does he point out the basis for classification?
3. Why does he not name each category in the first paragraph?
4. Why does he use numbers for each category? What is the basis for ordering the four categories?

The following shows the use of a sustained classification:

HERE IS NEW YORK

There are roughly three New Yorks. There is, first, the New York of the man or woman who was born here, who takes the city for granted and accepts its size and its turbulence as natural and inevitable. Second, there is the New York of the commuter—the city that is devoured by locusts each day and spat out each night. Third, there is the New York of the person who was born somewhere else and came to New York in quest of something. Of these three trembling cities the greatest is the last—the city of final destination, the city that is a goal. It is this third city that accounts for New York's high-strung disposition, its poetical deportment, its dedication to the arts, and its incomparable achievements. Commuters give the city its tidal restlessness, natives give it solidity and continuity, but the settlers give it passion. And whether it is a farmer arriving from Italy to set up a small grocery store in a slum, or a young girl arriving from a small town in Mississippi to escape the indignity of being observed by her neighbors, or a boy arriving from the Corn Belt with a manuscript in his suitcase and a pain in his heart, it makes no difference: each embraces New York with the intense excitement of first love, each absorbs New York with the fresh eyes of an adventurer, each generates heat and light to dwarf the Consolidated Edison Company.

The commuter is the queerest bird of all. The suburb he inhabits has no essential vitality of its own and is a mere roost where he comes at a day's end to go to sleep. Except in rare cases, the man who lives in Mamaroneck or Little Neck or Teaneck and works in New York, discovers nothing much about the city except the time of arrival and departure of trains and buses, and the path to a quick lunch. He is desk-bound, and has never, idly roaming in the gloaming, stumbled suddenly on Belvedere Tower in the Park, seen the ramparts rise sheer from the water of the pond, and the boys along the shore fishing for minnows, girls stretched out negligently on the shelves of the rocks; he has never come suddenly on anything at all in New York as a loiterer, because he has had no time between trains. He has fished in Manhattan's wallet and dug out coins but has never listened to Manhattan's breathing, never awakened to its morning, never dropped off to sleep in its night. About 400,000 men and women come charging onto the island each weekday morning, out of the mouths of tubes and tunnels. Not many among them have ever spent a drowsy afternoon in the great rustling oaken silence of the reading room of the Public Library, with the book elevator (like an old water wheel) spewing out books onto the trays. They tend their furnaces in Westchester and in Jersey but have never seen the furnaces of the Bowery, the fires that burn in oil drums on zero winter nights. They may work in the financial district downtown and never see the extravagant plantings of Rockefeller Center—the daffodils and grape hyacinths and birches and the flags trimmed to the wind on a fine morning in spring. Or they may work in a midtown office and may let a whole year swing round without sighting Governors Island from the sea wall. The commuter dies with tremendous mileage to his credit, but he is no rover. His entrances and exits are more devious than those in a prairie-dog village, and he calmly plays bridge while buried in the mud at the bottom of the East River. The Long Island Rail Road alone carried forty million commuters last year, but many of them were the same fellow retracing his steps.

The terrain of New York is such that a resident sometimes travels farther, in the end, than a commuter. Irving Berlin's journey from Cherry Street in the Lower East Side to an apartment uptown was through an alley and was only three or four miles in length, but it was like going three times around the world.

—E. B. White

1. What is White's basis for classification? Is it stated directly? What are his three New Yorks?
2. Since he discusses his third category in depth first, why didn't he state it as his first category?
3. Why does he devote the least space to his first category, and why is that category placed last?
4. What uses does White make of description, narration, and comparison?

EXERCISES

1. You are on a campus committee considering the fate of athletics during a time of budget cutbacks. The various committee members have divided the report into sections, and you are to explain the various kinds of athletic programs on campus, from intramurals through intercollegiate teams. Develop a way to classify all athletics on campus, and write your part of the report.

2. Another committee you serve on has asked your help preparing a brochure for new students. You have been asked to classify and explain the various kinds of housing available to students. Do so.

3. For the campus paper, you have decided to classify students on your campus in a way that makes fun of every type of student you can imagine. Invent a humorous way to classify students on your campus, and write the article.

4. For your autobiography, classify the roles you have played up to this point in your life and explain them.

5. For your autobiography, classify and explain your recreational activities.

6. At the beginning of each new television season, you like to provide your readers with a broad sense of the programming to be offered. Write an article for the campus newspaper classifying the kinds of programs offered on television.

7. Your major department has asked you to help prepare a handout for new majors indicating the kinds of careers available to graduates in your major. Write the handout.

Cause and Effect

The last of the designs for explaining concepts approaches argumentation. Writers often use cause-and-effect designs to *prove* something: "The *cause* of inflation is big government" or "The *effect* of reducing the size of the federal government will be lower inflation." Of course, not all cause-and-effect thinking contributes to persuasion, but the smoke of cause-and-effect thinking usually points to the fire of argument.

You probably sense already that causation creates a perpetual circle. Anything that happens is both a cause and an effect. A cue causes the cue ball to strike the nine ball. The effect of the cue ball hitting the nine ball is to cause the nine ball to sink in the pocket. But what effects follow? And what events caused the cue to hit the cue ball? Clearly, writing about causation requires drawing limits to what will be called *causes* and what will be called *effects*, and then sorting out the relationships between them. Approach an issue of causality by asking:

1. *What were the conditions when it occurred?* This returns you to the first of the flexible designs—description. By pointing out the features of a concept as it existed at a particular time, you can relate one feature to another.
2. *How did it come to be this way?* This returns you to the second of the flexible designs—narration. By spelling out the history of a particular concept, you can trace the relationship of one event to another.
3. *Is the cause enough to produce the effect?* A relationship between two things does not mean that one causes the other. If the Angels lose every time you watch them play, does your watching cause the team to lose? Oversimplification often damages causal reasoning, a subject we will say more about soon.

Precise causation can be impossible to establish. Rarely do we move with the exactness and precision of pure science. Instead we act on *probabilities*. If a person drives 100 miles an hour in the city, we think he will *probably* be stopped by the police. Seldom do we conduct experiments to test our notions of probabilities (or consequences). Instead, we prefer uncertainty to the possibilities of harm to ourselves or others. Even expert sharpshooters leave shooting apples from children's heads to the movies and to the William Tells of the world.

Although dealing with human beings denies us the certainties and precision of science, people are still amazingly predictable. A smile gets a smile in return. People form a line according to the order of their arrival. People do not always act according to prediction, but we become uncomfortable when they don't. We look for, and assume, predictability. A premise of this book is that surprises in organization confuse readers. In short, much of our lives depends upon what we perceive as predictable and probable.

As you may have noticed, discussions of causality can quickly become abstract and philosophical. We do not intend to journey any further into the nature of cause, but it is important to recognize that people have long wrestled with causality at the highest philosophical and religious levels. Our view of writing, however, is firmly rooted in the daily problems the world throws at us all. We leave ultimate questions for others and recommend instead the test of *utility*.

When trying to account for some present state of affairs, the writer engages in the search for causality; when trying to describe the outcome of a series of ongoing events, the writer attempts to predict effects. Understanding cause depends upon sifting the events of the past, while predicting effects looks to the future. For example, today's good weather was *caused* (past) by a high-pressure system off northern California; when a low-pressure system enters the region tomorrow, the *effect* will be (future) high winds and rains.

Establishing causality requires a writer to deal with facts. The problem comes in linking the facts to a specific effect. The first step in that linking process is to distinguish between causes that are *necessary* and causes that are *sufficient*. A *necessary* cause contributes to effect. It needs to be present for the effect to occur, but does not by itself guarantee the effect. A *sufficient* cause, however, is enough to cause the effect without anything else. Consider two examples:

1. A student confronts a professor over a grade. The student says "I don't deserve such a low grade because I studied hard and put in a lot of time on the material." How would the professor respond? One way might be to point out that for most people hard work and study are *necessary* to do well in a class, but they are not *sufficient*. They are among the things needed to produce the effect the student desires (high grade), but they are not enough by themselves.
2. Recently a young man sued his parents, charging them with neglect because he was "a failure in life." He said that his parents always gave him everything he wanted, that they never held him to any standard of behavior, and that their overindulgence at home made him incapable of performing satisfactorily in the world. The parents' lawyer might concede that the way his clients raised their son *contributed* to the way he turned out, but it was hardly the whole cause. The son has some responsibility for his own development, and other pampered children have turned out well. The parents' indulgence might have been *necessary* for the son to turn out as he did, but it was not *sufficient*.

Most cause-and-effect reasoning depends upon relating events in *time*. Go to a doctor with a set of symptoms, and the doctor will deal with them as effects. The diagnosis will link the symptoms to an earlier cause. (You might be told that grass pollens cause your running nose and itching eyes in the spring.) But it is easy to make mistakes in relating causes and effects. (The doctor's diagnosis might be right, but then again, something besides grass pollens might cause the same symptoms.) Do not expect cause A always to lead to effect B unless you know that the circumstances are precisely the same. Although you must depend upon probability, do not confuse it with truth.

Certain errors recur in reasoning from cause to effect or from effect to cause. Here are some guidelines:

1. Make sure that the cause is sufficient to produce the effect. Oversimplification harms far too many causal analyses. Be skeptical about seemingly simple causes for complex problems. Is it likely, for example, that governmental spending is *sufficient* to cause high inflation?
2. Never assume that there is only one cause for anything. Try to think of something that has only one cause. When you find something, ask what caused that cause. What you are today is certainly more than the effect your parents had on you. What about teachers, friends, and experiences? genetic coding? your mother's prenatal diet? your father's smoking?
3. Never assume that a cause will have a single effect.
4. Do not assume that event A causes event B because event A happened first. Just because the sun always sets after the "CBS Evening News," you cannot assume that the "CBS Evening News" causes the sun to go down. The two might be remotely related (the evening news is likely to be broadcast at a time near sundown), but that is not enough for a causal relationship. In other cases, something can "trigger" an event, but be only the last link in a causal chain. For example, a student might say that a failing grade from Professor Landwehr will lead to the student's academic suspension. All the student's previous failing grades, however, might have caused a situation in which Professor Landwehr's grade is the last of a chain of events leading to a suspension. In other words, do not think that the last straw alone broke the camel's back.

A Design for Causality

1. *Preparation.* Tell your reader the purpose of your causal analysis. Why do you wish to prove that one thing caused another? What will be accomplished by establishing a causal link? You might need to provide background. What, for example, led you to try to prove or predict something? Do key terms need to be defined so that your reader understands what you will describe?

2. *Expansion.* Developing a causal analysis resembles explaining a process. Cause and effect function in time since there must be some interval between a cause and its effect. Isolate the various steps of causation. What happened first, what second, what third, and what fourth? Begin each step by telling what happened and then explain the causal relationships. Your description and narration will provide the facts, and your explanation will sort out and establish the *meaning* of the facts. Recall the guidelines stated above when you explain the meaning of facts. While what you describe and narrate normally can be verified by others, your mind supplies all connections between events and all notions of meaning. It takes a searching and skeptical mind to trace causes and predict effects accurately.

3. *Closure.* Sum up all the causal links. After you develop several relationships between events, your reader needs to have the threads pulled together. Be sure that the reader understands the point of your analysis.

CAUSALITY

Preparation:
Tell your reader the purpose of your causal analysis.
Provide necessary background, including defining important terms.

Expansion:
Isolate each step leading from a cause to its effect.
Describe and narrate the events of each step, and then explain the meaning of each event using guidelines on causality.

Closure:
Sum up and explain the causal links developed in your expansion section.

Here is a single cause-and-effect paragraph from a larger essay:

Now, it is clear that the decline of a language must ultimately have political and economic causes: it is not due simply to the bad influence of this or that individual writer. But an effect can become a cause, reinforcing the original cause and producing the same effect in an intensified form, and so on indefinitely. A man may take to drink because he feels himself to be a failure, and then fail all the more completely because he drinks. It is rather the same thing that is happening to the English language. It becomes ugly and inaccurate because our thoughts are foolish, but the slovenliness of our language makes it easier for us to have foolish thoughts. The point is that the process is reversible. Modern English, especially written English, is full of bad habits which spread by imitation and which can be avoided if one is willing to take the necessary trouble. If one gets rid of these habits one can think more clearly, and to think clearly is a necessary first step towards political regeneration: so that the fight against bad English is not frivolous and is not the exclusive concern of professional writers.
—George Orwell, "Politics and the English Language"

1. What is the purpose of Orwell's causal analysis in this paragraph?
2. How many steps of causation does Orwell isolate?
3. Orwell's third sentence ("A man may take . . .") offers an analogy. What is the value of the analogy at this point?
4. How has Orwell's point been refined by the final sentence?

Here is an example of a fully developed causal analysis:

CARBON MONOXIDE POISONING

About 1846, I wished to make experiments on the cause of poisoning with carbon monoxide. I knew that this gas had been described as toxic, but I knew literally nothing about the mechanism of its poisoning; I therefore could not have a preconceived opinion. What, then, was to be done? I must bring to birth an idea by making a fact appear, i.e., make another experiment to see. In fact I poisoned a dog by making him breathe carbon monoxide and after his death I at once opened his body. I looked at the state of the organs and fluids. What caught my attention at once was that its blood was scarlet in all the vessels, in the veins as well as the arteries, in the right heart as well as in the left. I repeated the experiement on rabbits, birds and frogs, and everywhere I found the same scarlet coloring of the blood. But I was diverted from continuing this investigation, and I kept this observation a long time unused except for quoting it in my course *a propos* of the coloring of blood.

In 1856, no one had carried the experimental question further, and in my course at the Collège de France on toxic and medicinal substances, I again took up the study of poisoning by carbon monoxide which I had begun in 1846. I found myself then in a confused situation, for at this time I already knew that poisoning with carbon monoxide makes the blood scarlet in the whole circulatory system. I had to make hypotheses, and establish a preconceived idea about my first observation, so as to go ahead. Now, reflecting on the fact of scarlet blood, I tried to interpret it by my earlier knowledge as to the cause of the color of blood. Whereupon all the following reflections presented themselves to my mind. The scarlet color, said I, is peculiar to arterial blood and connected with the presence of a large proportion of oxygen, while dark coloring belongs with absence of oxygen and presence of a larger proportion of carbonic acid; so the idea occurred to me that carbon monoxide, by keeping venous blood scarlet might perhaps have prevented the oxygen from changing into carbonic acid in the capillaries. Yet it seemed hard to understand how that could be the cause of death. But still keeping on with my inner preconceived reasoning, I added: If that is true, blood taken from the veins of animals poisoned with carbon monoxide should be like arterial blood in containing oxygen; we must see if that is the fact.

Following this reasoning, based on interpretation of my observation, I tried an experiment to verify my hypothesis as to the persistence of oxygen in the venous blood. I passed a current of hydrogen through scarlet venous blood taken from an animal poisoned with carbon monoxide, but I could not liberate the oxygen as usual. I tried to do the same with arterial blood;

I had no greater success. My preconceived idea was therefore false. But the impossibility of getting oxygen from the blood of a dog poisoned with carbon monoxide was a second observation which suggested a fresh hypothesis. What could have become of the oxygen in the blood? It had not changed with carbonic acid, because I had not set free large quantities of that gas in passing a current of hydrogen through the blood of the poisoned animals. Moreover, that hypothesis was contrary to the color of the blood. I exhausted myself in conjectures about how carbon monoxide could cause the oxygen to disappear from the blood; and as gases displace one another I naturally thought that the carbon monoxide might have displaced the oxygen and driven it out of the blood. To learn this, I decided to vary my experimentation by putting the blood in artificial conditions that would allow me to recover the displaced oxygen. So I studied the action of carbon monoxide on blood experimentally. For this purpose I took a certain amount of arterial blood from a healthy animal; I put this blood on the mercury in an inverted test tube containing carbon monoxide; I then shook the whole thing so as to poison the blood sheltered from contact with the outer air. Then, after an interval, I examined whether the air in the test tube in contact with the poisoned blood had been changed, and I noted that the air thus in contact with the blood had been remarkably enriched with oxygen, while the proportion of carbon monoxide was lessened. Repeated in the same conditions, these experiments taught me that what had occurred was an exchange, volume by volume, between the carbon monoxide and the oxygen of the blood. But the carbon monoxide, in displacing the oxygen that it had expelled from the blood, remained chemically combined in the blood and could no longer be displaced either by oxygen or by other gases. So that death came through death of the molecules of blood, or in other words by stopping their exercises of a physiological property essential to life.

This last example, which I have very briefly described, is complete; it shows from one end to the other, how we proceed with the experimental method and succeed in learning the immediate cause of phenomena. To begin with I knew literally nothing about the mechanism of the phenomenon of poisoning with carbon monoxide. I undertook an experiment to see, i.e., to observe. I made a preliminary observation of a special change in the coloring of blood. I interpreted this observation, and I made an hypothesis which proved false. But the experiment provided me with a second observation about which I reasoned anew, using it as a starting point for making a new hypothesis as to the mechanism, by which the oxygen in the blood was removed. By building up hypotheses, one by one, about the facts as I observed them, I finally succeeded in showing that carbon monoxide replaces oxygen in a molecule of blood, by combining with the substance of the molecule. Experimental analysis, here, has reached its goal. This is one of the cases, rare in physiology, which I am happy to be able to quote. Here the immediate cause of the phenomenon of poisoning is found and is translated into a theory which accounts for all the facts and at the same time includes all the observations and experiments. Formulated as follows, the theory posits the main facts from which all the rest are deducted: Carbon monoxide combines more intimately than oxygen with the hemoglobin in a molecule of blood. It has quite recently been proved that carbon monoxide forms a definite combination with hemoglobin. So that the molecule of blood, as if petrified by the stability of the combination, loses its vital properties. Hence everything is logically deduced: because of its property of more intimate combination, carbon monoxide drives out of the blood the oxygen essential to life; the molecules of blood become inert, and the animal dies, with symptoms of hemorrhage, from true paralysis of the molecules.

—Claude Bernard

1. What is the purpose of Bernard's causal analysis? Is that purpose clearly indicated in the first paragraph? Is the purpose suggested in the first paragraph modified in the last paragraph?
2. What background does the first paragraph provide?
3. Identify the individual steps Bernard follows. Point to each significant theoretical discovery. How does he help the reader to understand causality at each stage?
4. What triggered the steps of Bernard's investigation? How did he know that his observations were *sufficient*?
5. What is the function of paragraph 4? What does it try to do with the content of the first three paragraphs?
6. Bernard's explanation is clearly scientific, but he uses the first person throughout. What is gained (or lost) by adopting this point of view?
7. Why does he say that he "could not have a preconceived opinion"?

EXERCISES

1. For a chapter in a junior high text, explain what causes a natural phenomenon (rain, clouds, tides, wind, hail).

2. For a brochure to be left as a courtesy in doctors' offices, explain what causes a particular ailment (asthma, hayfever, epilepsy, diabetes).

3. Which person in your life has had the greatest influence upon you? Write a letter to that person explaining the effect that he or she has had upon your life.

4. What single thing do you most wish you had not done in your life? For your autobiography, describe what you did and explain its effects.

5. A campus committee on which you serve has been charged with recommending a solution to a particular problem. (You choose the problem; it might be parking, poor security, inadequate housing, or a shortage of qualified teachers for your major.) Write the section of the committee's report that explains the causes for the problem and the effects it has on your school.

6. For your autobiography, isolate one of the traits of your character (honesty, laziness, curiosity) and explain how you came to possess that trait. Assume that environmental influences are more important than hereditary ones.

ARGUING POLICIES

Who has not been in an argument? Remember the rush of emotion, the certainty that you are right, the vain attempt to make the other person accept what you know is truth? *Argument* is probably not the right word for this sort of communication. How about "quarrel" or "dispute" or "wrangling"? Whichever word you choose, a distinction can be made between two ways of presenting positions on issues, and the word *argument* can be heard representing both approaches. The most familiar meaning of *argument* emphasizes the heated disagreements people enjoy. Let's call this *wrangling*. In the history of the word *argument*, the notion of wrangling came late to the scene, mostly in verbal contexts.

The more traditional meaning of *argument*, and the one we will use, focuses on the logical presentation of evidence to convince someone to accept a point. Of course, some arguments try to refute a point, but that is usually part of convincing a reader to accept a different point. In *argument*, as in athletic contests, writers depend upon a set of rules. Although no gaming commission spells out the rules for argument, centuries of practice have been passed on to each new generation of writers. Consequently, we ask that you put away any anticipation of approaching argument as a chance to climb barefisted into the ring to prove that you have the truth about abortion, the draft, or communism.

The Purpose of Argument

Argument shares with wrangling a common goal: to *convince* a reader. In both cases, someone wants another person to accept what he or she says (that is, to believe) or to do something (that is, to act). A person might try to persuade you to believe that a car accident was not his fault or that you should support "no-fault" car insurance in your state.

But argument involves convincing other people in quite different ways from wrangling. Winning is everything in wrangling. Someone must be a loser. How many wranglings have you heard that left the wranglers with their dignity or mutual respect? And how often has someone genuinely accepted the other's position instead of being cowed? Rarely does wrangling change minds. Instead, it arouses strong feelings, typically dividing people rather than leading them to some sort of common ground.

Argument, on the other hand, tries to avoid such results. It does so by a combination of rules (that we will look at shortly) and by relying upon all the other designs for writing we have looked at so far. Each design contributes to a foundation of understanding between writer and reader that prepares for argument. *Description* leads to an understanding of what something looks like. *Narration* contributes to an understanding of what happened in a series of events. But we pointed out earlier that writers rarely describe or narrate for the sake of doing so. Both description and narration contribute to understanding within the designs for *explaining concepts*. In turn, the designs for explaining concepts lead to understanding. Readers grasp concepts through comparison, classification, and causality. Seeing things in relationship to other things promotes understanding between writer and reader.

But notice: *understanding does not require agreement*. We can understand what someone says, understand a concept, understand evolution, understand a president's foreign policy—we can understand all these things without agreeing with them. But unlike wrangling, *argument* assumes that no agreement can come without the foundation of understanding. If people cannot agree on facts or circumstances, they scarcely can go on to agree on what the facts or circumstances mean, or what ought to be done about them.

Argument consequently promotes respect for the opposition, and rightly so. No one argues about an issue without a strong case to be made for *both* sides. At one time people argued over whether the earth is flat or round. Does that issue still have two sides? Do we argue over whether to allow people to fly in airplanes? Obviously not. Instead, we argue about issues such as prison reform, environmental protection, nuclear power, and social security. People on both sides of these issues offer persuasive, reasonable arguments. While a person who wrangles can ignore the quality and quantity of the opposition's arguments (and can therefore never reach the level of understanding, much less of agreement), traditional argument leads a writer to establish first a basis for mutual understanding and to respect the opposition throughout the writer's own argument.

Assumptions

One reason a writer must respect an opposing argument is that his or her argument makes assumptions. Awareness of assumptions encourages tolerance. What if something you assume should turn out untrue? For example, what if you assume that most people on welfare can work but are too lazy, but your reader knows that a careful investigation has revealed that 95 percent of those receiving welfare are physically not capable of performing normal tasks?

It is impossible for anyone to think without assumptions. Sometimes writers knowingly make assumptions and tell their readers that they are doing so. ("Assuming that Israel genuinely wants peace ....") Often, however, people have beliefs—assumptions treated as truths—that cannot be proven factually or demonstrated logically. Does athletics build character? Does success in business depend upon hard work? Whether or not such statements are true, people strongly believe that they are and state or imply them as truths rather than as assumptions.

In arguing, be aware of the assumptions you make, and qualify statements based upon assumption. Test for assumptions by asking whether a statement is a *fact*, an *inference*, or an *opinion*. A *fact* can be verified. Facts reside in the world we can observe and thus know with the certainty of the senses. Tests can be applied—of measurement, of time, of occurrence, of definition, and so on. We can all look at a stopwatch and agree that the watch shows that 12.2 seconds has elapsed. We can measure 100 meters for a race course. We can agree that it is a fact that Bob Smith ran the 100-meter race today.

An *inference* can be drawn when factual evidence points to something being true but not enough evidence exists to establish the statement as a fact. If you see someone shivering, you might *infer* that the person is cold. It is a fact that the human body shivers at a certain stage of being cold. But the person might be shivering because he is upset. While it is a fact that the person shivered, it is not a fact that he shivered because he was cold unless you can establish the causality. Similarly, we infer that certain things will happen: the sun will rise tomorrow; a traffic fatality will occur each day in the United States. These things are likely, but not true until they happen. Inference depends upon probability. Enough evidence can be assembled to suggest that something is probably true, but not enough to establish that thing as fact.

Opinion is something we believe to be true but for which not enough evidence exists to establish it as fact or inference. A person believes that rubbing a gold ring on a stye will cure it. Not enough evidence exists to establish this as a fact. Any testimonial ("it worked for me") lacks the controls to establish inference. One cannot communicate without making assumptions and without having beliefs. The difficulty comes in attempting to ignore facts or inferences that might contradict a belief or an assumption.

Ethos

The way in which a writer presents himself or herself can be as important as the argument itself. Would you believe someone who sounds ignorant? How would you react to a writer who says, directly or indirectly, "I have never studied the musk ox, nor have I any experience with the animal, but I think it is safe to say that the species has little importance to the welfare of mankind"?

The face a writer shows a reader is called *ethos*. Sometimes expertise furnishes the basis for ethos. If a person sounds expert or has credentials in a subject, a reader will probably give weight to that person's assertions. But a voice of reason will probably do more to

The following essay presents an argument relying heavily on **ethos***. Notice especially the elements of organization and the relationship of* **ethos** *to those elements.*

THE AGONY OF TRYING TO TELL MY CHILDREN

*Problem +
list of
subtopics*

> *This is the time of the Jewish New Year, yet it feels more like Passover to me. My children are asking me four questions: Where, when, why, how?*
> *Earlier this week, my son Josh asked me where Lebanon was and when the killing began. His sisters wanted to know how it could ever have happened, and why Jewish soldiers had let it happen. They wanted to know what had become of us as a people.*

*Background
establishing
personal
element of
ethos*

> *They know that their paternal grandparents came to the United States to escape the pogroms, and reminded me of a story I always told about my grandmother. On my grandmother's 85th birthday, my aunt wanted to take her to see "Fiddler on the Roof" as a present. When my grandmother saw the tickets, she burst into tears. She said that she could never see that lighthearted musical when the memories of the horrors that her family had experienced in Bialystok still kept her awake at night.*

*Restatement
of purpose
with per-
sonal ethos*

> *My children wanted to know how it was possible that the people who had experienced or were heir to the horrors of the ghettos and the concentration camps could have the slightest part in the murders in Beirut.*

Ethos

> *I tried to answer them. I have been crying over Lebanon, and feel powerless in a way that I never felt during the civil-rights movement and the Vietnam War. It was easy to tell my children*

Subtopic 1

> *where the sad country of Lebanon is located and to describe the complex Christian, Palestinian and Israeli interests that led to such an explosion of hatred. It was also easy to tell them*

Subtopic 2

> *when the killing began, though even that is a more complex question that might require knowledge of hundreds and even thousands of years of conflict.*

*Expanded
version of
subtopic 3*

> *But to answer the third and fourth questions, the bitter ones, what do I say to my children? Why were unarmed and defenseless people slaughtered? Why, as Josh put it, do people do these things to each other? What is the nature of hatred? Why do people kill for ideological or religious reasons?*

Speculative answer to subtopic 3

It's hard when you don't have answers to your children's moral questions. Yet I don't understand how people who are probably loving parents and loyal friends turn themselves into murderers. All I can say to my children and myself is that human beings whose lives are miserable can reach a point of forgetting their humanity. A child can torture animals or become a bully out of personal misery. Adults, too, find cruel ways to work out their own hurts.

Doubting that answer to suggest the complexity of the issue

My children weren't convinced—and I'm not either—by this or any other explanation. I've heard about what enables people to torture and kill. We are a deficient species, and obviously need to grow morally. My children don't want to look at the pictures of the bodies in Lebanon, and I can't look at them without feeling that life is so delicate and so meaningless that it may simply rest on a chemical error doomed to self-destruction.

Subtopic 4

But the hardest question, the fourth kasher, is how could the massacre in Lebanon have happened, how could Israeli soldiers have let armed killers into the camps? It is the same question that has been asked of the "good Germans." How could they have allowed the concentration camps to have happened, and how could they not have known what was happening?

Rephrasing the subtopic through analogy

Extending the analogy

The same question must be asked of the American Jewish community. Knowing what we know of the consequences of the invasion of Lebanon, how can we remain silent? How can the major representatives of the American Jewish community continue to defend every action of Israel?

Emphasis on ethos: the moral man struggling to answer a difficult question

I cannot tell my children how the massacre in Lebanon was possible. Nor can I give them moral reassurance that people are good at heart and that love and justice are overriding forces in the world. Christians and Jews and Arabs were involved in the negation of love and the debasement of justice in Lebanon. The best I can say is that some kinds of ideological obsessions drive people to treat others as not human.

Concluding with moral stance: what the single individual can do in such circumstances.

I can't answer all four questions for my children, and I don't believe that fasting and repenting this Yom Kippur will eliminate the sins of this year. As Jews and as people, we must repudiate massacre and arbitrary violence, whatever their source. The answer that I have to give to my children is that I choose to speak out against hatred without fully understanding it, and strive for justice without knowing whether it will ever be achieved.

—Herbert Kohl

gain a reader's respect than anything else. If the writer sounds like a fair-minded, thoughtful, informed person, the reader will accept the writer's arguments more readily than if the writer sounds overbearing or conceited or ignorant. The content might be the same in both cases, but the tone emerging from the sentences can strongly affect the reader.

The Golden Rule adapts well to argument: Treat your reader as you would want your reader to treat you. Business writers call this "you-attitude." If you seem sensitive to your reader's situation (if it is important) and if you respect your reader's intelligence and judgment, that reader will probably extend the same respect to you. You can't smile when you write, but you can find verbal equivalents. Good *ethos* does not persuade your reader to accept your point, but it does create an atmosphere in which your reader will listen attentively and respectfully to your argument.

Foundations for Persuasion

If you compare two backpacks, you will emphasize their relationship. Your explanation will lead your reader to a greater understanding of each. Argumentation will pick up the results of the comparison to convince a reader to select a particular backpack. Argument shifts the focus from understanding to persuasion. The writer might leave intact the comparison of the two backpacks, but that comparison would be placed in a framework leading to the writer's point: "For the McKinley expedition, the Chinook backpack should be chosen over the Denali." The word "should" characterizes argument. The writer wants the reader to accept or to act upon what the writer says. Let's consider the two main kinds of *shoulds:* standards and values. The first kind of argument appeals to objective standards. If something can be weighed, counted, timed, or measured, the writer uses such standards to prove a case. Consider the kinds of tests that could be performed on a backpack: weight, metal strength, fabric strength, endurance to stress, and so on. The details related to objective standards persuade a reader that one backpack should be preferred to another.

The second kind of argument appeals to *values*. Humans function sometimes in contradictory ways when dealing with values. People react in terms of *morality* or of *expediency*.

Morality appeals to a higher law. It asserts that people agree that certain things in the culture are good, honest, or true. The writer points out the particular moral agreement (e.g., beating horses is wrong) and then leads to his *should* (e.g., the president of the company that makes Denali backpacks beats his horses; therefore Chinook backpacks should be purchased). The appeal to morality often tries to reach the reader's emotions and therefore requires care by the writer. Dr. Johnson was aware of the misuses of this appeal when he said that "Patriotism is the last refuge of a scoundrel."

Expediency appeals to the reader's self-interest. People care about their wealth and their security. If a writer can show how the reader can gain by accepting the writer's *should*, most readers listen. For example, a writer might point out that the maker of Chinook backpacks provides a 20-percent discount to the McKinley expedition in addition to a free stuff-sack for every pack purchased.

However, such appeals do not work out this neatly in real argument. Life would be pleasant if some clear standard or value could be set up and used to reach agreement. A clear standard cuts off the need to convince when the standard is clearly applied. If agreement exists on the strength standards for backpacks for the expedition and agreement that only those standards will be used, then no persuasion will be needed for agreement on selection of the backpack. (Although persuasion might be needed to establish agreement on the standards.)

Even more confusing can be disagreements springing from the relationship between morality and expediency. For example, many argue that nuclear power should be developed quickly. Basing their argument on expediency, they say that the power is needed, that the country must become independent of foreign oil, and that the need outweighs any risks. Those opposing nuclear power also argue on grounds of expediency, saying that nuclear power is not practical or cost-effective. But the real core of their opposition is fear of possible harm to themselves and their children from radiation or the consequences of nuclear disaster to themselves, their children, and their community. This is a moral argument (the higher good of the family and community) tinged with self-interest (fear of personal consequences).

Arguments of morality often intertwine with arguments of expediency, apparently because human beings convince themselves that what is in their best interest is also what is right. As a writer, pay close attention to arguments you offer that seem purely moral to you because your reader might pick up the core of self-interest that you miss. In short, don't get in the position of the American officer in Vietnam who said that it was necessary to destroy a village in order to save it.

Time Frames for Argument

While time seems to be the province of narrative, arguments can be distinguished by their time: *present, past,* and *future.* While arguments might be conducted in the *present* tense, few arguments can be about what happens *now.* Once a *now* occurs, it joins the past tense. But some arguments do belong to the present tense because they are timeless. They focus neither on what did happen or what ought to happen, but on issues rising above such considerations. Such arguments focus on universal truths: love of parents, honor, respect for legitimate authority, loyalty, or honesty. People argue such issues primarily in ceremonies, such as funerals or graduation speeches. These arguments remind us of important values—communal and personal—rather than attempt to establish the meaning of an event or what should happen in the future.

Traditionally, arguments about the *past* have been called *forensic.* They attempt to uncover facts (what happened) and assemble them in order to reach some conclusion about their significance. The argument might focus upon a person's guilt or innocence, or upon the outcome of a military battle. While some trial lawyers might depend upon their powers of persuasion when facts are not on their client's side, most arguments about the past disappear when the facts become available. If two people can agree upon the facts, upon what actually happened, argument usually ends.

Most arguments focus on the future. Called *deliberative rhetoric* by the ancients, arguments about the future occur any time we contemplate the future consequences of present events or consider what policy might be best. Arguments about the future tend to rely on expediency, looking foward to what is possible or impossible. Usually people can agree more easily on the goal rather than on the means to realize the goal. For example, people probably will agree that their nation ought to be secure, but will argue about the means that will best assure this security. Of course, not all arguments about the future focus on means (such as arguments about laws governing abortion), but most do.

Fallacies

Consideration of the strategies of argument inevitably concentrates on warning writers about pitfalls. Our discussion of common appeals has already strayed into warnings about their misuse. Aristotle furnished a list of the errors in thinking that those who argue need to avoid, and two thousand years later we still rely on his list. Fallacies confuse arguments and prevent understanding. Some writers unconsciously fall into fallacies, and others use them intentionally. Those who intentionally present fallacies try to win agreement by cheating. Chief among the abusers are certain politicians and advertisers—those who seek agreement with their side in any way they can get it.

Fallacies presented in books, such as this one, look so simple and foolish that it seems hard to imagine a sensible writer using them or a thoughtful reader accepting them. Not so. The more emotional a writer gets about his or her subject, the more likely he or she will fall prey to fallacies. Readers behave the same way. A person emotionally drawn into an argument can easily be persuaded by fallacious reasoning. Subjects dear to a person's heart make even the most intellectually mature person lose detachment and accept fallacious arguments. That makes it a good rule to avoid disputes on such subjects as religion, politics, or morals. (Unfortunately, some people like to argue—or wrangle—about little else.)

Fallacies come under three general headings: *faulty language, faulty relationship,* and *diversions.* We do not pretend to present an exhaustive list of fallacies. By pointing out key fallacies, though, we hope to begin to cut a clear trail over some confusing terrain.

Faulty language fallacies cause much confusion in argument. Generally, language goes wrong in three ways:

1. *Loaded language.* Many words trigger emotional responses. Followers become "toadies." The opposition become "jerks." People get labeled with racial or sexual terms. Of course, completely objective language remains an ideal, but writers can choose words to minimize a reader's emotional reaction. Bias in language can lead a reader to question the writer's ethos.

2. *Abstract and technical language.* You might raise an eyebrow if someone says, "Let's interface during lunch, and I'll give you some input on how that impacts the project." Such language pervades our speech. We even heard a minister asking people during a Sunday church service to bow their heads and pray for "Divine Input." Writ-

ers need both technical and abstract words, but much judgment needs to accompany their use. That judgment needs to take into account the reader's ability to comprehend the terms and whether the words will convey a writer's choice more clearly than simpler or more concrete words. Inflated language can also cause negative interface with your reader, impacting your ethos situation and its reaction syndrome.

3. *Vague language.* Except for proper names, all words can be vague. But some words convey more precise meanings than others. *Yellow* is more precise than *lightly colored. Canary yellow* specifies the meaning even more. But words do not fit on a neat scale, inviting the writer to snatch the most concrete choice at the scale's end. Instead, *context* determines what is concrete and what is vague. Find the most precise word for the meaning you intend to convey. The rhetorical situation governs word choice. Once you recognize the level of word choice appropriate for a reader (that is, the kinds of words that will lead to a reader *understanding* you), avoid shifting level.

A particular kind of vague language comes from quotations taken out of context. Consider, for example, the often-quoted maxim, "Don't let your right hand know what your left hand is doing." Often people seem to use it to suggest plunging ahead, confused or not. But the originator of the quotation, St. Matthew, had a different meaning in mind. Recounting the words of Jesus in the Sermon on the Mount, St. Matthew admonishes against excessive pride in religious practices. He suggests that a chief difference between the Old Law and the New Law is that the reward for giving alms lies in the giving, not in the praise a person receives for doing it. When using quotations, be certain that you accurately reflect the meaning their authors' intend.

Faulty relationship fallacies pretend that a logical relationship exists between two things. The writer tries to persuade through the implications of the relationship. Here are three varieties:

1. *Post hoc.* Most people still use the Latin name for this common fallacy. *Post hoc* (short for *post hoc, ergo propter hoc*—"after this, therefore causing this") is a fallacy of causation. It happens when writers assume that coincidental relationships in time are causal relationships. A broken leg on a Friday the thirteenth might lead a superstitious person to see causality between the date and the accident. Any time an argument asserts that one event caused another

simply because that event preceded the other, that argument commits the *post hoc* fallacy.

Post hoc seems obvious, but writers fall into it easily. People seem especially prone to *post hoc* thinking in politics: "Americans fought in two World Wars right after electing Democratic presidents" or "Within a year after our budget passed, interest rates came down." Once people commit themselves to a position they look for reasons to support that position. Whatever seems to cause the results they want or to cause events they object to, people grab for support.

Watch for *post hoc* thinking whenever you assert causality. Ask whether the relationship is real or coincidental. If it is real, ask whether the cause is sufficient. (See p. 132 for a discussion of necessary and sufficient causes.) Instead of advancing a partial cause as a whole cause, point out honestly the degree to which you see causality at work. Your honesty will aid ethos and give a sense of balance to your argument.

2. *Wholes and parts.* A person commits a fallacy when he says that he knows that Lambda Gamma is a rich girls' sorority because the three girls he knows in the sorority are rich. What is true of the parts of something is not necessarily true of the whole. Because some politicians are crooked, it is not reasonable to assert that politicians in general are crooked. Those with prejudices toward other races, religions, or social groups depend upon such thinking when defending their prejudices.

The opposite kind of thinking—that what is true of the whole is also true of the parts—also creates fallacies. For example, "He can't be a bad doctor because he graduated from State University and it has the best medical school in the world." What is true of a large unit does not necessarily become true of that unit's components. A good speaker system might have mediocre cross-overs. A first-rate team need not be composed entirely of first-rate players.

3. *Non sequitur.* Another Latin phrase, *non sequitur*, means "it does not follow." Such fallacies occur when a conclusion does not necessarily follow from the evidence or reasoning that has gone before. In many ways, all fallacies are *non sequiturs* since they offer conclusions not validly reached. This category provides a home for a large number of fallacies not worth naming individually. Advertising typically depends on the effective use of *non sequiturs*. Pay attention to the logic of ads to sharpen your ability to recognize this kind of fallacy.

Diversionary fallacies occur when someone tries to convince others by avoiding the key issues or by focusing upon some minor part of an argument. Such efforts to divert a reader might seem obvious when pointed out, but they often succeed through strong emotional appeal. Here are three types of *diversionary fallacies:*

1. *Ad hominem.* This fallacy occurs when a person ignores the argument and attacks a person instead. (*Ad hominem* is Latin for "to the man.") Trials—fictional and real—often show lawyers attacking the character of a witness rather than the witness's testimony. Such attacks assume that juries will not believe or will discount the testimony of those whose characters have been called into question. Such tactics pervade political thinking, as people label and damn proposals from people and parties on the basis of who does the proposing rather than what the proposal contains.

This fallacy prevents a fair evaluation of a proposition. By raising emotion (such as a person's prejudgments about a particular party or politician), understanding gets bypassed in the writer's drive for agreement. Some writers intentionally divert attention from the substance of the argument through *ad hominem*, probably because they fear that understanding the issue might lead to an agreement the reader is predisposed against. It is hard to fall into *ad hominem* accidentally. A writer knows when he or she focuses upon a person's character rather than upon the core of an argument.

2. *Bandwagon.* People fear being left out. Despite assertions about individuality, people wear Calvin Klein jeans, drive Porsches, and drink Perrier because advertisers convince people that they will be left out otherwise. (Some advertisers even offer the doublethink that a person acquires individuality by joining the group purchasing a product.) As does *ad hominem*, the bandwagon fallacy diverts attention from the substance of an argument and preys on people's emotions and fears. Writers know when they misuse such emotional appeals, and discerning readers often spot the fallacy. Bandwagon works much better for a speaker, who can toy with an audience's emotions, than for a writer, who knows that a reader has time to think and question.

3. *Inappropriate emotional appeals.* While *ad hominem* and bandwagon count for a large portion of the diversionary fallacies, a significant variety of emotional appeals exists. Writers can flatter, pity, ridicule, pretend to be "just folks," or play on prejudice. All these approaches ignore the question at hand, projecting an argument into

emotional realms. With attention diverted to emotional responses, a person cannot focus his or her mind on the issues central to an argument.

All diversionary fallacies turn the reader from the key issue to emotional side issues. Some writers use such fallacies intentionally, hoping to win agreement without having to reach understanding. Chief among the abusers of these fallacies are propagandists—politicians, advertisers, or those seeking converts to a cause. However, readers often see through the deception of such arguments, and the writer loses *ethos* when that happens.

You need to be aware of such abuses to recognize when an opponent is not arguing by the rules and to catch yourself if you start to use such arguments. Saying that assumes, of course, that you intend to argue ethically. We focus intentionally on ethical argument only. The spirited exchange of ideas and thoughts leads to growth and learning. The fallacies mislead, and a person uses them because of a lack of intellectual discipline or outright deceit. Often people believe that arguments are something one must win. We believe that when one learns, one wins. The center of good argument is understanding, and fallacies prevent understanding.

While ethical argument avoids fallacies, the center of argument does not lie in what to avoid, but in how to present argument. Rembering that much of the content of argument is exposition, let us consider the two major kinds of reasoning that contribute to the designs for *arguing policies:* reasoning through connections and reasoning through examples. While arguments often mix the two strategies, it is useful to recognize the separate processes of each.

Reasoning Through Connections

Some reasoning can be valid, but not true. Sound contradictory? Consider the following reasoning: "All Pinto drivers are reckless; Brendan drives a Pinto; therefore Brendan is a reckless driver." The conclusion—that Brendan is a reckless driver—is valid. If the first two statements are accurate, the third logically follows. But we might not accept the conclusion as true if we know just one Pinto driver who is not reckless or if we doubt the premise that all Pinto drivers are reckless. Although Brendan drives a Pinto, he is not necessarily reckless.

Reasoning through connections often leads to such problems. Connective reasoning asserts that a conclusion can be drawn based upon a set of propositions. The weight of such arguments lies in the propositions. If they are valid, according to connective reasoning the conclusions must also be valid. The syllogism is the classic form of such reasoning:

All men are mortal.

Socrates was a man.

Therefore, Socrates was mortal.

A person advancing such an argument pays close attention to the propositions (called premises in formal logic). Connective reasoning assumes that everything needed to reach a conclusion lies in the propositions. Everything needed to prove Socrates is mortal can be found in the two premises.

The normal reaction to such connective arguments is to doubt the premises, and that is precisely the weakness of connective arguments. As long as the conclusion follows from the premises, one cannot question whether the conclusion is valid. But one can question whether it is true by questioning the premises. Because connective arguments assume that they include all evidence necessary to reach a sound conclusion, they can seldom be found in the issues argued about in real life. Such arguments usually take up residence in logic courses, and learning the form of these arguments provides excellent mental discipline.

However, one form of connective reasoning often can be found in the arguments advanced by writers: *if–then reasoning*. Rather than assume certainties in propositions, if–then reasoning emphasizes possibilities that might lead to a conclusion. This kind of argument contains an *if* statement expressed hypothetically: "*If* alternative sources of energy are found, Saudi Arabia's influence in the world will decline." As with other connective arguments, this one assumes that the conclusion validly follows from the proposition. But it does not assert the propositions in a way that insists or implies that they are true.

If–then reasoning shows up in arguments because writers typically deal with possibilities rather than with certainties. (Certainties occur at the level of understanding.) Formulating policies, strategies, or plans usually requires seeing several possibilities taking place and understanding in detail the potential consequences of various assumptions or sets of conditions.

Actual if-then wording can be found most readily in oral statements: "If I walk out in the rain, then I'll get wet" or "If I study hard, then I'll have a better chance of earning an 'A' in chemistry." While many written sentences contain if-then phrasing, a larger pattern of if-then reasoning can provide a basis for organizing major portions of arguments, or even whole arguments. A writer will explain a set of circumstances and then consider what the circumstances imply. This reasoning suggests that if kinds of information are correct then a conclusion can be reached about their meaning or about what ought to be done about them.

Consider the following propositions and the resulting conclusion:

If the Smarts campus has only 500 parking spaces, and

If certain land can be purchased for parking spaces, and

If money exists to purchase the land, and

If money exists to build the parking lot, and

If no other considerations prevent building the parking lot, then

Smarts University should build a new parking lot.

A writer would try to establish the correctness of each proposition through evidence. If all seems in order, the conclusion simply follows from the propositions. Notice that this argument contains a section focusing on "other considerations." It makes sense to anticipate the kinds of issues that seem peripheral but might be used to refute an argument.

A Design for Connective Arguments

1. *Preparation.* First state the problem that you will address and then indicate in general terms the action or agreement you seek. Provide any background that will help the reader to follow your argument, such as historical information or definitions of key terms.

2. *Expansion.* Offer your propositions in a sensible order (e.g., in

order of increasing importance or of logical relationship). Since you will present each proposition as an "if," be sure to provide ample evidence that is correct. You will need to reach understanding with your reader on each proposition. Apply carefully the designs for explaining concepts. For example, to establish an "if" part of an argument, you might use comparison and contrast to show that one piece of land is superior to another for a new parking lot on the Smarts campus.

As you move from proposition to proposition, be consistent in the ways you present and treat information, and present propositions impartially. Your approach might be expedient (propositions focusing on someone's best interests) or moral (focusing on what is right). Be sure to anticipate any objections your reader might have to your propositions.

3. *Closure.* Because connective arguments emphasize the propositions, your conclusion will probably not need elaborate attention. It will follow logically from what you have stated and supported in your propositions. Restate in specific terms the action or agreement

---

CONNECTIVE ARGUMENTS

PREPARATION:

  State the problem.
  Indicate in general terms the action or agreement you seek.
  Provide background as needed.

EXPANSION:

  Offer propositions in logical order.
  Present propositions consistently and impartially.
  Use the designs for explaining concepts to reach understanding with your reader on each proposition.
  Anticipate objections to your propositions.

CLOSURE:

  Be sure that your conclusion is stated clearly and derives logically from your propositions.
  Restate in more specific terms the action or agreement you seek.
  Your conclusion need not be long.

you seek. Be sure that your conclusion is clear and that it derives directly from your propositions.

Identify the if-then reasoning in the following articles:

LABOR-MANAGEMENT TEAMWORK CAN CREATE NEW PROSPERITY

President Reagan, the man whom almost all union leaders regard as their implacable foe, may ultimately be a source of revitalization for organized labor in this country.

Historically, hard times have often spurred union growth as workers unite their forces to battle the devastation of unemployment. That happened most dramatically in the Great Depression, when millions of workers joined unions with the encouragement of laws passed by a sympathetic New Deal Congress, led by President Franklin D. Roosevelt.

The country now is in its most severe economic downturn since those Depression days, and, if there is no recovery within the next several months, workers could once again begin turning to unions for help.

At best, this prospect puts the union leaders in an uncomfortable position. They are worried that their predictions of more economic misery under Reagan may come true because, if they do, all Americans—including union members—will suffer.

But if a recovery is slow in coming, and is hastened by a reversal of Reagan's supply-side, "trickle-down" theories, the unions could make major gains.

Obviously, the unions would lose credibility, if not large numbers of members, in a Reagan Prosperity. The unions would survive such a prosperity, of course, but the odds are that they will thrive if Reagan fails.

The first real test of whether labor's fortunes are changing will come in the November election. In 1980, labor suffered one of its most serious political defeats in modern history when, despite an all-out effort, not only was Reagan elected President but also Republicans took control of the Senate, and many long-time labor supporters lost seats in the House.

Union leaders throughout the country are using this Labor Day to open their campaign to help elect a more sympathetic Congress, and they are doing it by denouncing the President's programs—which, they insist, are largely responsible for the recession. The unions charge Reagan with hypocritically offering up a federal budget containing the largest deficit in history while simultaneously offering a constitutional proposal to mandate a balanced budget.

They charge him with being a "rich man's President," and they believe that his Republican colleagues will go down to defeat this fall in the barrage of criticism that they are directing at Reagan and his supporters.

If the labor-backed Democrats make significant gains in November, union membership won't increase automatically, but the political climate will be more favorable for the unions— a climate created at least in part by the unity that the unions have achieved in their nearly unanimous opposition to Reagan.

For unions to make membership gains, however, it may be necessary for them to offer workers something more than a vehicle for opposing the conservative economic policies of the President, and something more than so-called "business unionism" that just helps protect jobs and helps members hold onto (if not raise dramatically) the increases in wages and fringe benefits that unions have won over the years.

That "something more" might be a new system of collective bargaining that would put the unions in the forefront of the growing movement to reduce the traditional adversary relations between workers and corporate managers.

Unions today are more willing to accept the notion of greater labor-management cooperation and a sharing of power and responsibility with corporate executives.

But they seldom lead the movement for industrial democracy, often leaving its leadership to innovative managers who want to follow the cooperative route. Many times, companies appear to adopt a facade of cooperation with workers only as a device to keep the union idea away from employees, hoping that workers will believe that they have a voice in company management. In fact, they are being manipulated as part of an anti-union campaign.

At other times, however, companies seem sincere, and the result is not just more worker-management cooperation but also a non-union firm. One well-known example is Motorola. Its full-page ads laud its success in competing with the Japanese in electronics because of its "participative management attitude."

Motorola's goal is to make every employee an effective part

of the management team—a system that it says creates enthusiasm, dedication and attention to details by all employees.

Unions could increase their own capacity for leadership by taking the initiative in a drive for worker-participation programs and for industrial democracy that, its promoters argue, offers workers more than the essential but unimaginative concept of "business unionism" that concentrates only on the basic goals of winning wage and fringe-benefit improvements.

Another potential for increasing unions' strength is their minimal role in the management of pension funds, which already total nearly $900 billion. Many union officers argue that, since the money set aside for workers' retirement belongs to the workers, they and their unions should at least help decide how to invest the pension funds. But, so far, unions have failed to assert themselves in those massive investment decisions.

If, by their failure, the Reagan economic policies create a more pro-union climate in the country, and the unions promote what many of them concede are exciting, innovative ideas of industrial democracy and pension power for workers, the near future could bring about a resurgence of union strength.

And perhaps, through such labor-management cooperation, the unions and their counterparts in management could help create the kind of prosperity that they so firmly contend this Labor Day might come about with the end of "Reaganomics."

—Harry Bernstein

1. What problem does Bernstein mention in the first paragraph? What action or agreement does he seek?
2. What is the function of the second paragraph?
3. What does paragraph 4 achieve? Why does it appear after paragraphs 2 and 3? Could the article start as effectively with paragraph 3?
4. Pinpoint the if-then argument of the first three paragraphs. Do you expect this if-then argument? What signals give you such an expectation?
5. Trace each if-then argument used in this article. (Do not expect each to use "if-then" phrasing.) Do you detect a particular order?
6. Which designs for *explaining concepts* does this article subordinate to the if-then argument?

7. Does Bernstein anticipate objections to his propositions?
8. Does Bernstein's conclusion follow logically from his propositions? Does his closure restate more specifically the idea he stated in the first paragraph?

AWAY WITH BIG-TIME ATHLETICS

At their mid-January annual meeting, members of the National Collegiate Athletic Association were locked in anguished discussion over twin threats to big-time college athletic programs: rapidly rising costs and federal regulations forcing the allocation of some funds to women's competition. The members ignored, as they always have, the basic issue concerning intercollegiate athletics. That is the need to overhaul the entire bloated, hypocritical athletic system and return athletics to a sensible place in the educational process.

A complete overhaul of the athletic programs, not the fiscal repair now being attempted by the NCAA, is what is necessary. For decades now big-time football, and to a lesser degree basketball, have commanded absurdly high priorities at our colleges and universities. Football stands at the center of the big-time system, both symbolically and financially; the income from football has long supported other, less glamorous sports.

Many American universities are known more for the teams they field than for the education they impart. Each year they pour hundreds of thousands of dollars apiece into athletic programs whose success is measured in games won and dollars earned—standards that bear no relation to the business of education and offer nothing to the vast majority of students.

The waste of resources is not the only lamentable result of the overemphasis of intercollegiate athletics. The skewing of values is at least as damaging. Everyone involved in the big-time system—players, coaches, alumni and other boosters, school officials, trustees, even legislators—is persuaded that a good football team is a mark of the real worth of an educational institution. Some of the most successful coaches elevate that bizarre notion to a sort of philosophy. Woody Hayes of Ohio State has said that the most important part of a young man's college education is the football he plays. Jim Kehoe, athletic director at the University of Maryland, has said of the games played by Maryland: "You do anything to win. I believe completely, totally, and absolutely in winning."

Anyone doubtful of the broad psychic satisfaction provided by winning teams need only observe who it is that shouts, "We're number one!" It is seldom the players and only sometimes other students. The hard core of team boosters is composed of middle-aged men—mainly alumni but also legions of lawyers, doctors, and businessmen with no tangible connection to the school.

In the South, where football mania rides at a shrill and steady peak, winning seems to offer a special reward: an opportunity to claim the parity with other regions that has been so conspicuously lacking in more important areas of endeavor. In Alabama in the late sixties, when Coach Bear Bryant was fielding the first of his remarkable series of national championship teams, both Bear and team were the objects of outright public adulation: that is, *white* public adulation. White Alabamians, reacting to the assaults on George Wallace and other bastions of segregation, took a grim, almost vengeful pride in "their" team. During those years, when I covered the South as a reporter, one could hardly meet a white Alabamian who didn't talk football or display, on an office or den wall, a picture of Bryant and the Crimson Tide squad.

The disease of bigtime-ism seems to run rampant in provincial places where there is little else to do or cheer for: Tuscaloosa and Knoxville, Columbus and Lincoln, Norman and Fayetteville. But everywhere, always, it feeds on a need to win—not just win a fair share of games but win almost all of them, and surely all of the "big" ones.

At the University of Tennessee last fall, coach Bill Battle nearly lost his job because the Volunteers won a mere seven out of twelve games. Never mind that Battle's Tennessee teams had previously amassed a five-year record of forty-six victories, twelve defeats, and two ties and had been to a bowl in each of those years. Although Battle was eventually rehired, he received no public support from a university administration which seemed to agree with the fanatics that, outstanding as his record was, it was not good enough.

Everyone knows something about the excess of recruiting high-school players and something about the other trappings of the big-time system: the athletic dormitory and training table, where the "jocks" or "animals" are segregated in the interests of conformity and control, the "brain coaches" hired to keep athletes from flunking out of school; the full scholarships ("grants in aid"), worth several thousand dollars apiece, that big-time schools can give to 243 athletes each year. (Conference regulations restrict the size of football traveling squads to about sixty, while the NCAA permits ninety-five players to be on football scholarships. This means that some three dozen football players at each big-time school are getting what's called a full ride without earning it.)

What few people realize is that these are only the visible workings of a system that feeds on higher education and diverts it from its true purposes. The solution, therefore, is not to deliver slaps on the wrist to the most zealous recruiters, as the NCAA often does, or to make modest reductions in the permissible number of athletic scholarships, as it did last year. The solution is to banish big-time athletics from American colleges and universities.

Specifically, we should:

1. Eliminate all scholarships awarded on the basis of athletic ability *and* those given to athletes in financial need. Every school should form its teams from a student body drawn there to pursue academic interests.

2. Eliminate athletic dormitories and training tables, which keep athletes out of the mainstream of college life and further their image as hired guns. Also eliminate special tutoring, which is a preferential treatment of athletes, and "red shirting," the practice of keeping players in school an additional year in the hope that they'll improve enough to make the varsity.

3. Cut drastically the size and the cost of the coaching staffs. Football staffs at Division I schools typically number twelve or fourteen, so that they are larger than those employed by professional teams. With practice squads numbering eighty or fifty, the present staff size creates a "teacher–pupil" ratio that permits far more individualized instruction on the playing field than in the classroom. The salaries paid to assistant coaches should be spent to hire additional faculty members. The salaries of head coaches, who in some states earn more than the governor, should be reduced to a point where no head coach is paid more than a full professor.

4. Work to eliminate all recruiting of high-school athletes. It has produced horrendous cases of misrepresentation, illegal payments, and trauma for the young men involved.

The worst of the abuses is the athletic scholarship, because it is central to all the others. If members of a college team are not principally athletes, there is no need to lure them to the school by offering special treatment and platoons of coaches. They should be students to whom football or basketball is the season's major extracurricular acitvity.

What will happen if these changes are made? The games will go on. In fact, they may well be more like real games than the present clashes between hired, supertrained, and sometimes brutalized gladiators. Will the caliber of play suffer? Of course, but every school will be producing the same lower caliber. Given a certain proficiency, which the best of any random selection of student-athletes always possesses, the games will be as competitive and as exciting for spectators as they are today. Is a 70-yard run by a nonscholarship halfback less exciting than the same run by Bear Bryant's best pro prospect? For spectators who crave top athletic performance, it is available from a myriad of professional teams. We need not demand it of students.

Certainly, the counter-argument runs, alumni and other influential supporters would not stand for such changes. There would indeed be ill feeling among—and diminished contributions from—old grads who think of their alma mater primarily as a football team. Let them stew in their own pot of distorted values. Those legislators whose goodwill toward a state university depends on winning seasons and free tickets can stew with them. A serious institution is well rid of such "supporters." They may discover the pleasures of a game played enthusiastically by moderately skilled students who are not in effect paid performers.

Will athletic-program revenues drop? They undoubtedly will, at least for a while; not many people will pay seven dollars to see games of admittedly lower quality, nor will the TV networks pay fancy fees for the right to televise them. The fans and the networks will eventually return, because these will be the only college games available. And think of the financial savings, as the costs of the typical big-time athletic program drop by hundreds of thousands of dollars a year. If a revenue gap persists, let it be made up out of general funds. The glee club, the intramural athletic program, and innumerable other student activities do not pay for themselves. Why should intercollegiate athletics have to do so?

Supporters of big-time programs often say piously that, thanks to those programs, many young men get a college education who otherwise would have no chance for one. That is true. But there are even more young men, of academic rather than athletic promise, who deserve whatever scholarship money is available. If somebody has to pay an athlete's way to college, let it be the professional teams that need the training that college competition provides.

The president of a good Southern university once told me privately that he would like to hire outright a football team to represent his school and let the educational process proceed. George Hanford of the College Entrance Examination Board, who has made a study of intercollegiate athletics, would keep the present system but legitimize the preparation of players for professional sports. Hanford would have a college teach athletes such skills as selecting a business agent and would permit student-athletes to play now and return later to do the academic work required for a degree.

While Hanford's suggested changes would remove the mask of hypocrisy from big-time college athletic programs, they would not solve the fundamental problem: the intrusions the programs make on the legitimate functions and goals of an educational institution. For institutions with a conscience, this problem has been persistently vexing. Vanderbilt University football coach Art Guepe summed it up years ago, when he characterized Vanderbilt's dilemma as "trying to be Harvard five days a week and Alabama on Saturday."

Because of pressures from alumni and others who exalt the role of football, Vanderbilt is still attempting to resolve this dilemma; and it is still failing. Now it is time for all the Vanderbilts and all the Alabamas to try to be Harvard whenever they can and Small-Time State on Saturday.

—Roger M. Williams

1. What problem does Williams mention in the first paragraph? What action or agreement does he seek?
2. What is the function of the second paragraph?
3. What is the function of paragraphs 3 through 10? Do you detect a method for organizing these paragraphs? Could they be placed as effectively in a different order? Could other issues be raised, replacing those raised in paragraphs 3 through 10, without affecting what goes before and after these paragraphs?

4. What is the effect of the four points Williams puts forth in the middle of the article (paragraphs 11 through 14)? What is the logic tying these paragraphs to those preceding?

5. Notice the specific examples of if-then reasoning in the remainder of the article. How are these cases of if-then reasoning tied to the first fourteen paragraphs?

6. Does Williams's conclusion follow logically from what has gone before? What specific action or agreement does he want? How has Williams refined the purpose indicated in the first paragraph?

7. What is Williams's narrative stance: expert or novice? participant or observer? How does his narrative stance differ from Bernstein's in the preceding article?

8. What is the basic appeal in this article: expediency, morality, or something in between?

9. Does Williams make any assumptions that cause you to have reservations about his proposals?

10. Does Williams anticipate counterarguments? Are there any that he omits?

11. How *practical* is his argument? Can it be taken seriously?

EXERCISES

1. Use the problem with parking on the Smarts campus (p. 154) as the basis for preparing a connective argument to support building a new parking lot. Make up specific evidence to support each "if" section.

2. Return to Exercise 3 of "Fixed Designs" (p. 79). Write that letter again, using if-then reasoning.

3. Using if-then reasoning, prepare a letter to your representative in Congress convincing him or her to take a stand on a particular political issue (nuclear power, disarmament, military spending).

4. For budgetary reasons, the president of the college has decided to eliminate the major in your field. She has arranged to have all students in your major admitted to a good college nearby, although one with a somewhat less prominent reputation. A committee of students in your major has formed to appeal the president's decision. On behalf of the committee, write to the president using if-then reasoning.

5. The local school board where you went to high school has banned several books from the school's shelves. Among the books are *Huckleberry Finn, The World According to Garp*, and *Catcher in the Rye*. Take a position on this issue and write a letter to the editor of your local paper arguing in support of your position. Use if-then reasoning.

6. Your student government is considering sponsoring a Day of Protest over some pressing issue (nuclear power, disarmament). The event is expected to draw over ten thousand people since a prominent rock star has promised to perform at the rally. A college across the state attempted a somewhat similar event two years ago, and reportedly the crowd behaved irresponsibly and damaged parts of the campus. Some on your campus favor the event, and some oppose it. The president must decide whether to allow the event. You have kept well informed about the issue from the beginning and head a group taking a definite stand (for or against, you choose). On behalf of your group, write to the president supporting or opposing the Day of Protest.

7. Select a topic that raises strong emotions but about which you believe you can maintain an open mind even though you have taken a stand on it (abortion, required prayer in schools, the death penalty, nuclear power, the draft). Use connective reasoning to argue a position, but argue the position *opposite* to the one which you believe.

8. Using connective reasoning, write a letter to a recognizable historical person (Napoleon, Joan of Arc) urging that he or she *not* follow the course of action that eventually led to his or her downfall.

Reasoning Through Examples

Reasoning through connections seeks certainty. It implies that valid propositions lead to valid conclusions. But *reasoning through examples* persuades by presenting *probability*. Like building blocks, examples pile up evidence leading to a generalization:

Mr. Smith has written five essays in his English class.

Mr. Smith has serious problems with spelling.

Mr. Smith has serious problems with sentence structure.

Mr. Smith has a very limited vocabulary.

Apparently, Mr. Smith has a poor background in English.

Each piece of information contributes to the generalization that Mr. Smith has a poor background in English. But other generalizations could be offered based on the same evidence. For example, one might say that Mr. Smith will probably fail his composition course. But despite the evidence, Mr. Smith might not be doing poorly in his English course because he has a poor background. He might have a learning disability. (That is, his background might have been quite good, but dyslexia prevents him from recognizing written symbols.) Or he might have had emotional problems when he wrote the five essays. Or his teacher might have been incompetent. The point? Any generalization reached through examples must be tentative. Other conclusions could be reached. To assert without qualification that "Mr. Smith has a poor background in English" would not fairly represent the limitations in the evidence.

Although *reasoning through examples* offers uncertainty, it represents the way in which our minds usually work. Most argument depends upon examples. Such thinking is less tied to rules than is connective thinking and relies on language, rather than on formal logic, to establish probability or truth. Examples appeal to experience. If they make sense to a reader, he or she will accept them as support for an argument.

Two kinds of examples support arguments: *personal* and *interpreted*. *Personal examples* provide evidence in raw form. In ordinary, everyday observation we see details and events that lead to conclusions about people, nature, or whatever. No one interprets the evidence for us. We decide what it means. Two tests govern such evidence: Is it *adequate* and is it *typical?* If your first romantic affections led to your being jilted, it would be unreasonable for you to generalize that all men or women are untrustworthy. Similarly, it would be a mistake to contend that Democrats oppose social welfare programs because you discovered that ten Democrats are so opposed. In both cases the evidence was neither adequate nor typical. Not only was there not enough evidence to make such generalizations, but the evidence did not reflect what a person would normally find. More experience might lead a person to the opposite conclusion.

Interpreted examples come from other people—experts, witnesses, acquaintances. The test of adequacy also applies to interpreted evidence: Is the interpreted evidence enough to prove the argument? But two more tests must be added: *bias* and *reliability*. If you wish to present interpreted examples, be sure that an authority is actually qualified to speak on the subject. You have probably noticed how advertisers like athletes or models to argue for shampoo and beer. Are these people qualified to testify to a product's superiority? Of course, written arguments are not advertisements, but a writer needs to verify an expert's credentials. And expertise in one area (e.g., engineering nuclear reactors) does not establish authority in a related area (e.g., nuclear disposal) or a distant area (e.g., nuclear warfare).

In addition to establishing *reliability* through an authority's qualifications, consider an authority's *bias*. Is the person providing the interpreted evidence committed to a position through prejudgments, or is he or she open to new evidence and to various ways of looking at the evidence? Are the person's interpretations or language slanted in a particular way? Use of interpreted evidence can reflect on the writer's own ethos.

Reasoning through examples usually goes wrong in one of three ways: jumping to conclusions, using unreliable testimony, and offering false analogies. Let us consider each.

1. *Jumping to conclusions.* If you develop an earache right after eating an apple, clearly it is unfair to conclude that apples cause you to have earaches. But how much evidence is enough? If the same thing happens three times in a row, should you conclude that apples cause your earaches? Knowing when the evidence is enough always presents writers with a challenge. Practice provides the only answer. Experience furnishes a sense of what will convince without excess. Offering evidence requires judgment. Consider the quality and the quantity of evidence. Be skeptical both about evidence and about those who provide it. When you draw conclusions, ask whether the evidence is both adequate and representative.

2. *Unreliable Testimony.* Readers evaluate specific pieces of evidence primarily in terms of reliability and bias. Does your presentation suggest that the personal evidence you present is reliable? What about your interpreted evidence? Reliability can be considered in two

ways: actual reliability and perceived reliability. Actual reliability requires accurately presenting all facts, information, and quotations. If you provide an incorrect fact or if you quote someone inaccurately, you call your own argument into question.

But it is not enough to present information accurately. The reader must perceive that you do so. Clearly a reader who perceived actual error will doubt you. But so will one who perceived that you *might* be in error. Such perceptions occur for many reasons, not all of which you can control. For example, you might not quote a particular authority because that authority has nothing relevant to say on the point, but nevertheless a reader might suspect your motives for not mentioning this authority. Consider all necessary information, and then look at that information with an objective eye to see whether your presentation seems reliable, especially to an unsympathetic reader.

Readers also look for *bias*. Do you or those whose evidence you present seem to have something to gain or seem so emotionally committed that evidence might not get fair treatment? Not all self-interest should be criticized, but a person can be aware of the existence of self-interest. For example, it makes sense when purchasing a new car to consider the relatively unbiased information in consumer periodicals over the statements of a salesperson. If you know that you are biased in favor of or against something, you can still present reliable evidence in an impartial way. When you recognize your own biases, you can alert your reader. Your honesty will not necessarily work against your argument. You will preserve the ethos of an honest person. But if your reader senses that you are unaware of your bias or that you deliberately slant evidence, you may lose your reader's respect.

One last point about evidence. It should be current, especially in scientific and technical matters. New evidence comes to light. One authority replaces another by having more reliable information. In some cases, tried and proven testimony must be combined with new considerations of a subject. Subjects vary in the kinds of evidence available, but you should always look for the most accurate evidence available.

3. *False Analogy*. Often reasoning uses analogies as particular kinds of examples. Instead of a specific instance, you might wish to show that something is like something else. Scientific thinking often uses analogy, proposing, for example, that if certain forms of life are

found in certain habitats, similar forms of life might be found there as well. Such reasoning can open up new possibilities. Analogical reasoning relies on comparison, and the comparison may or may not be valid. As with other forms of reasoning through example, the goal of analogy is probability. Analogies do not assert truth, but relationship and possibility. Rarely do analogies directly advance an argument, but they do contribute an important kind of reasoning when combined with other evidence.

All arguments using examples depend upon providing enough evidence to make probable the truth of a generalization. Do not fear the uncertainty of this sort of argument. Life rarely gives us clear-cut truths, and genuine arguments have such complexity on each side that you can never feel certain that your argument presents truth. Instead, you can only hope to have approached some sort of truth.

A Design for Reasoning by Example

1. *Preparation.* State the problem that your argument will address and indicate your main point. Choose between two strategies in stating your main point: indicate a general direction for the argument (the indirect approach) or tell the reader precisely what you will prove (the direct approach). Because argument presupposes that your reader needs convincing, you might wish to present and weigh evidence before spelling out a precise position. Instead, you will guide the reader carefully through the evidence, leading to a clear statement of your position at the end of the discourse. For example, an indirect introduction to an argument about the death penalty might say, "Critics have long debated the value of the death penalty." By the last paragraph, a precise point can be made: "The death penalty should be reinstated to save the taxpayers of Massachusetts the expense of keeping murderers in prison." In other cases, however, you might wish to state your position clearly at the beginning. The decision about when to state your position must be made in terms of the effect each kind of argument will have on your reader. Following an indication of your main point, provide any background that will help the reader to follow your argument.

2. *Expansion.* Present each point in an order that makes sense. You might choose to offer your most persuasive points first, or you may build to a statement of your position. Often the subject matter contains a recognizable logic for developing your points. When you gather evidence to support a generalization, you might notice pieces

of evidence starting to interrelate. The pieces of evidence will fall into a pattern that leads logically to a generalization. In presenting an argument to a reader, the reverse process occurs. A typical paragraph will present a generalization, and the evidence (which fits together to form that generalization) will follow.

Some arguments advance by simply offering one point after another. Others advance by offering various points and then bringing those points together for discussion later in the argument. Such discussions might weigh the points in terms of morality or in terms of expediency. Ask why the points interweave to make something appear bad or good or why the points interweave to make a course of action seem prudent, unwise, beneficial, or practical. At every stage, you will need the designs for exposition, description, and narration to lead your reader to understanding.

3. *Closure.* If you elected an indirect approach, make your position clear. If you have chosen a direct approach, restate your position if

---

REASONING BY EXAMPLE

PREPARATION:

   State the problem.

   Indicate your main point, choosing between a direct and an indirect approach.

   Provide useful background.

EXPANSION:

   Present each point in a sensible order.

   Use the designs for description, narration, and exposition to reach understanding with your reader.

   If useful, bring major points together for discussion once they have been presented.

CLOSURE:

   For the indirect approach, make your position clear.

   For the direct approach, restate your position if necessary.

   Summarize key arguments, if useful.

   Be as brief as possible.

you think that it will help to convince your reader. In stating or restating your main point, you might find it helpful to bring together the key points of your argument. But avoid oversimplifying or over-stating your conclusion. After leading a reader to an understanding about individual points through exposition and then persuading that reader to accept your view of the subject, you may harm your case with a tactless conclusion. Be as subtle as possible.

The following shows an indirect approach using a single example:

THE RIGHT TO DIE

The world of religion and philosophy was shocked recently when Henry P. Van Dusen and his wife ended their lives by their own hands. Dr. Van Dusen had been president of Union Theo-logical Seminary; for more than a quarter-century he had been one of the luminous names in Protestant theology. He enjoyed world status as a spiritual leader. News of the self-inflicted death of the Van Dusens, therefore, was profoundly disturbing to all those who attach a moral stigma to suicide and regard it as a violation of God's laws.

Dr. Van Dusen had anticipated this reaction. He and his wife left behind a letter that may have historic significance. It was very brief, but the essential point it made is now being widely discussed by theologians and could represent the beginning of a reconsideration of traditional religious attitudes toward self-inflicted death. The letter raised a moral issue: does an individ-ual have the obligation to go on living even when the beauty and meaning and power of life are gone?

Henry and Elizabeth Van Dusen had lived full lives. In recent years, they had become increasingly ill, requiring almost con-tinual medical care. Their infirmities were worsening, and they realized they would soon become completely dependent for even the most elementary needs and functions. Under these circumstances, little dignity would have been left in life. They didn't like the idea of taking up space in a world with too many mouths and too little food. They believed it was a misuse of medical science to keep them technically alive.

They therefore believed they had the right to decide when to die. In making that decision, they weren't turning against life as the highest value; what they were turning against was the notion that there were no circumstances under which life should be discontinued.

An important aspect of human uniqueness is the power of free will. In his books and lectures, Dr. Van Dusen frequently spoke about the exercise of this uniqueness. The fact that he used his free will to prevent life from becoming a caricature of itself was completely in character. In their letter, the Van Dusens sought to convince family and friends that they were not acting solely out of despair or pain.

The use of free will to put an end to one's life finds no sanction in the theology to which Pitney Van Dusen was committed. Suicide symbolizes discontinuity; religion symbolizes continuity, represented at its quintessence by the concept of the immortal soul. Human logic finds it almost impossible to come to terms with the concept of nonexistence. In religion, the human mind finds a larger dimension and is relieved of the ordeal of a confrontation with non-existence.

Even without respect to religion, the idea of suicide has been abhorrent throughout history. Some societies have imposed severe penalties on the families of suicides in the hope that the individual who sees no reason to continue his existence may be deterred by the stigma his self-destruction would inflict on loved ones. Other societies have enacted laws prohibiting suicide on the grounds that it is murder. The enforcement of such laws, of course, has been an exercise in futility.

Customs and attitudes, like individuals themselves, are largely shaped by the surrounding environment. In today's world, life can be prolonged by science far beyond meaning or sensibility. Under these circumstances, individuals who feel they have nothing more to give to life, or to receive from it, need not be applauded, but they can be spared our condemnation.

The general reaction to suicide is bound to change as people come to understand that it may be a denial, not an assertion, of moral or religious ethics to allow life to be extended without regard to decency or pride. What moral or religious purpose is celebrated by the annihilation of the human spirit in the triumphant act of keeping the body alive? Why are so many people more readily appalled by an unnatural form of dying than by an unnatural form of living?

"Nowadays," the Van Dusens wrote in their last letter, "it is difficult to die. We feel that this way we are taking will become more usual and acceptable as the years pass.

"Of course, the thought of our children and our grandchildren makes us sad, but we still feel that this is the best way and the right way to go. We are both increasingly weak and unwell and who would want to die in a nursing home?

"We are not afraid to die . . . . "

Pitney Van Dusen was admired and respected in life. He can be admired and respected in death. "Suicide," said Goethe, "is an incident in human life which, however much disputed and discussed, demands the sympathy of every man, and in every age must be dealt with anew."

Death is not the greatest loss in life. The greatest loss is what dies inside us while we live. The unbearable tragedy is to live without dignity or sensitivity.

—Norman Cousins

1. Does Cousins state the problem in the first paragraph?
2. Does Cousins provide background?
3. How important are description, narration, and exposition to Cousins's argument?
4. How does Cousins use his central example to argue his point? Point to the various subtopics of his argument.
5. Would Cousins's argument be strengthened by using several examples rather than a single example? Is it reasonable to come to a judgment on the basis of a single example, even if it is an example of the quality of the Van Dusens' action?
6. Why does Cousins wait until the closure to state his main point? How might a reader's response be affected by a direct approach?
7. Read carefully the first sentence in paragraph 9. Whatever your response, select examples to formulate an argument supporting or opposing the argument that suicide can be justified as an act of free will.
8. If you were to write an essay adopting the argument you make in step 7, what inherent problems in arguing moral or ethical issues would you face?

The following shows a direct approach using several examples:

COP-OUT REALISM

On all sides, one sees evidence today of cop-out realism—ostensible efforts to be sensible in dealing with things as they are but that turn out to be a shucking of responsibility.

Example: Until fairly recently, off-track betting was illegal in New York State. Gambling on horses was regarded as a disguised form of stealing, run by professional gamblers who preyed upon people who could least afford to lose. Also outlawed was the numbers game, in which people could bet small amounts of money on numbers drawn from the outcome of the day's horse races.

Attempts by government to drive out the gambling syndicates had only indifferent results. Finally, state officials decided that, since people were going to throw their money away despite anything the law might do to protect them, the state ought to take over off-track betting and the numbers racket.

It is now possible to assess the effect of that legalization. The first thing that is obvious is that New York State itself has become a predator in a way that the Mafia could never hope to match. What was intended as a plan to control gambling has become a high-powered device to promote it. The people who can least afford to take chances with their money are not only not dissuaded from gambling but are actually being cajoled into it by the state. Millions of dollars are being spent by New York State on lavish advertising on television, on radio, in buses, and on billboards. At least the Mafia was never able publicly to glorify and extol gambling with taxpayer money. And the number of poor people who were hurt by gambling under the Mafia is miniscule compared to the number who now lose money on horses with the urgent blessings of New York State.

A second example of cop-out realism is the way some communities are dealing with cigarette-smoking by teenagers and pre-teenagers. Special rooms are now being set aside for students who want to smoke. No age restrictions are set; freshmen have the same lighting-up privileges as seniors.

The thinking behind the new school policy is similar to the "realism" behind New York's decision to legalize off-track betting and the numbers game. It is felt that since the youngsters are going to smoke anyway, the school might just as well make it possible for them to do it in the open rather than feel compelled to do it furtively in back corridors and washrooms.

Parents and teachers may pride themselves on their "realism" in such approaches. What they are actually doing is finding a convenient rationalization for failing to uphold their responsibility. The effect of their supposedly "realistic" policy is to convert a ban into a benediction. By sanctioning that which they deplore, they become part of the problem they had the obligation to meet. What they regard as common sense turns out to be capitulation.

Pursuing the same reasoning, why not set aside a corner for a bar where students can buy alcoholic beverages? After all, teenage drinking is a national problem, and it is far better to have the youngsters drink out in the open than to have them feel guilty about stealing drinks from the cupboard at home or contriving to snatch their liquor outside the home. Moreover, surveillance can be exercised. Just as most public bars will not serve liquor to people who are hopelessly drunk, so the school bartender could withhold alcohol from students who can hardly stand on their feet.

It is not far-fetched to extend the same "reasoning" to marijuana. If the youngsters are going to be able to put their hands on the stuff anyway, why shouldn't they be able to buy it legally and smoke it openly, perhaps in the same schoolroom that has been converted into a smoking den?

We are not reducing the argument to an absurdity; we are asking that parents and teachers face up to the implications of what they are doing.

The school has no right to jettison standards just because of difficulties in enforcing them. The school's proper response is not to abdicate but to extend its efforts in other directions. It ought to require regular lung examinations for its youngsters. It ought to schedule regular sessions with parents and youngsters at which reports on these examinations can be considered. It ought to bring in cancer researchers who can run films for students showing the difference between the brackish, pulpy lungs caused by cigarette smoking and the smooth pink tissue of healthy lungs. The schools should schedule visits to hospital wards for lung cancer patients. In short, educators should take the U.S. Surgeon-General's report on cigarettes seriously.

In all the discussion and debate over cigarette smoking by

children, one important fact is generally overlooked. The fact is that a great many children *do not* smoke. The school cannot ignore its obligation to these youngsters just because it cannot persuade the others not to smoke. It must not give the non-smokers the impression that their needs are secondary or that the school has placed a seal of approval on a practice that is condemning millions of human beings to a fatal disease.

Still another example of cop-out realism is the policy of many colleges and universities of providing common dormitories and common washrooms for both sexes. The general idea seems to be that it is unrealistic to expect young people not to sleep together. Besides, it is probably reasoned, if people are old enough to vote they are old enough to superintend their own sex habits. So, the thinking goes, the school might just as well allow them to share the same sleeping and toilet facilities.

The trouble with such policies is that they put the school in the position of lending itself to the breakdown of that which is most important in healthy relations between the sexes—a respect for privacy and dignity. No one ever need feel ashamed of the human body. But that doesn't mean that the human body is to be displayed or handled like a slab of raw meat. Sex is one of the higher manifestations of human sensitivity and response, not an impersonal sport devoid of genuine feeling. The divorce courts are filled to overflowing with cases in which casual, mechanistic attitudes toward sex have figured in marital collapses. For the school to foster that casualness is for it to become an agent of de-sensitization in a monstrous default.

The function of standards is not to serve as the basis for mindless repressive measures but to give emphasis to the realities of human experience. Such experience helps to identify the causes of unnecessary pain and disintegration. Any society that ignores the lessons of that experience may be in a bad way.

—Norman Cousins

1. Does Cousins state the problem in the first paragraph? Can you identify his main point? What would be the effect of starting with the second paragraph?
2. Does he provide useful background?
3. To what extent does Cousins rely on description, narration, and exposition to present each example?

4. List his examples on a sheet of paper. Do they appear in any particular order? Would you change the order if you were writing the essay?

5. What is the difference between the way Cousins uses examples in this essay and the preceding one?

6. Does he anticipate objections that might be raised against him?

7. In each example, Cousins suggests that a policy has been established because of erroneous assumptions. Upon what assumptions is each policy based?

8. How does Cousins's closure modify or refine the point he began with? How do the examples support that modification or refinement? What would be the effect of moving the last paragraph to the beginning?

EXERCISES

1. In the past year, you have noticed and read about problems with dogs running loose in your neighborhood. Write a letter to the city council convincing it to enact (or enforce) a leash law. Use a direct approach in reasoning by example.

2. As president of your college, you have been receiving complaints from local citizens about what happens when rock concerts are held on campus. Also, your own staff has reported many incidents in which campus property has been damaged or destroyed during or after the concerts. Write a memo to the student senate convincing its members that the present policies governing rock concerts must be changed and recommend the specific changes you think the senate should consider. (Even though, as president, you have the power to enforce the changes you want, you believe that students should govern certain affairs as long as they prove they can do so responsibly.)

3. Because of the problems stated in Exercise 2, the president has canceled all rock concerts indefinitely, including the six concerts scheduled for the rest of the year. Using the indirect approach (because his position has been declared), try to convince him to change or modify his position. Reason by example.

4. Find an advertising campaign that you find offensive or

distasteful and write a letter to the company's president convincing him or her to end the campaign.

5. A sun spot two years ago created a phenomenon that scientists have just documented as fact: the average life span on earth has been increased by ten years. You serve on a committee advising the president of the United States on what to do about the changes this phenomenon will bring. Select one area of public policy that must be changed because of this phenomenon and prepare a convincing argument for a particular change.

6. The trustees have proposed raising tuition by three times what it has been. Convince them that a lesser increase would be best. Be sure to take into account the circumstances that led them to propose an increase.

7. In an essay, argue for or against the following proposition: "The purpose of education is to produce people who will behave in predictable ways."

8. Urge a policy that is morally reprehensible but "necessary." (That is, argue expediency over morality.) Your challenge is to weaken the force of moral arguments by showing the overwhelming necessity of the policy. For example, you might argue that it is necessary to cheat to get into medical school.

3

Closure: Finishing Up

Closure leads to two actions: surveying what you have written and ending the discourse.

Rewriting

Whether you have written a five-hundred-word theme or a twenty-page report, all the pieces are not together until you reach the end. You begin with a purpose in mind. Where do you end? Naturally, you hope to end with your purpose achieved. But the act of writing often modifies original intentions. Writing not only asserts, but leads to discovery. Often a new sense of a subject comes from the act of writing about it.

What do you do when you reach the end of a first draft and discover that you have changed course? What do you do at the end of any first draft? Rewrite! A romantic notion still lingers (mostly among those who write little) that for some people writing comes easy. A brilliant first draft rolls from the typewriter. Not so. Or at least not so in any sort of frequent or predictable way. Good writing means rewriting. As you near the end, perhaps before attempting to write your *closure*, look back over what you have done. Consider again your purpose and identify the spots that need recasting in order to achieve your purpose.

To help you with this process, here are some questions to apply to the various designs:

I. The Fixed Designs
   A. Can the main point be stated clearly and concisely? What changes would you make in the main point?
   B. Is the design simple and clear?
   C. Will the reader understand what you say?
   D. Is the information complete? Is it examined thoroughly?
   E. Are assumptions stated?
   F. Is your purpose clear at the end?
   G. Do conclusions follow from what is presented?
   H. Do conclusions lead to reasonable recommendations?

II. Describing Objects
   A. *Accuracy of detail* is the primary consideration. Have enough details been presented to achieve the visual image of the object that you want? Of the details presented, have the *significant* ones been emphasized? When reading the description over, are you conscious of any *omissions* that ought to be included?
   B. Since it is rare that any object is described solely for itself, is it clear *why* the description is being given? If not, perhaps it is best to *state the purpose early*.
   C. Is there a recognizable *order* in the description? A reader should not be disoriented by any shift, either in *point of view* or in order of details presented. The maintenance of *perspective* is very important. Focus on *transitional devices*—how you get from one part of the description to another.
   D. Is the description *complete?* By this, we mean "Does it create the impression of completeness?" Has anything been left out? Does the description as it stands make a *satisfying whole?* If not, recheck first point C and then point B.
   E. Read the entire piece over one last time. Does it create the *effect* you intended? Is it objective? Do you *exaggerate* or

overwrite in order to produce a certain effect? (Check all adjectives.) Is it too literal? too detailed? too sentimental?

III. Narrating Events

   A. Again, the key issue at the beginning is *accuracy*. Have you presented enough *details?* Are all the details presented *relevant?*

   B. What is the *purpose of the narrative?* It has been said that we *argue* about the future (what we should do), but we *inquire* about the past. Narratives are most often presented for a purpose, and the purpose is usually to illustrate or render more believable some general point. Does your narrative do these things?

   C. Is the narrative *connected* and *consistent?* A narrative must be connected from beginning to end, and the point of view must be consistent. Not only must the narrative be connected to itself, but it must be connected to whatever general point you intend to make.

   D. Is the narrative *complete?* If you are narrating an event that is completed, is it clear from the narrative? If the event is not yet over, have you picked a reasonable place to pause? Have you made sure that the connections and conclusions you have drawn are *tentative?*

   E. Does the narrative establish a clear *balance between detail and controlling ideas?* Is so much detail presented that the point of the discourse is lost? A good way to look at this is in terms of *distance;* have you moved sufficiently away from the details of the narrative that it can be perceived as a whole (or, at least, as a whole up to a particular point in time)?

   F. What is the *link* between the narrative presented and the present? Are you drawing a parallel?

IV. Explaining Concepts

   A. The central problem in most writing about ideas and concepts is poor organization. It is difficult to move from concrete to abstract and back again. In describing objects and narrating events, space and time give order to most written discourse. In writing about concepts, the writer must perceive or impose an order, and the order must be *recognizable.*

B. Equal in importance is the question of *purpose*. This is sometimes called the *thesis,* or *controlling idea.* The controlling idea is the glue that holds writing on concepts together. Every paragraph of the discourse, in one way or another, must relate to the controlling idea of the discourse as a whole. Check each paragraph. Be able to state explicitly to yourself what its purpose is.

C. Make sure that all like items are presented in groups and that the basis for grouping is clearly understood and indicated.

D. If the concept being presented is very complex and difficult to understand, have the *major points* and *subpoints* been presented in the preparation section? Most readers appreciate any attempt by writers to help them keep their bearings, especially when the going is difficult. Has the orientation been as *brief* and *to the point* as possible? Remember, the idea or concept you are about to present will be difficult enough. Don't confuse matters by presenting an overly long orientation section.

E. Is a *summary* necessary? Many writers summarize mechanically. Make a judgment. If you have oriented properly, and have done the other things mentioned, a summary is often not necessary. Worse, some readers will take it as an insult.

V. Arguing Policies

A. Assume that *accuracy, order,* and *completeness* are essential.

B. Is the *significance* of the material to be presented emphasized at the beginning? It is often a good idea, before the deliberative portion of the discourse even begins, to emphasize early the importance of what is to follow.

C. Is the method of argument appropriate to the *subject matter* and *audience?*

D. Be very demanding in judging the *quality* of the *examples* brought forward. Apply the same high standard of judgment to whatever other forms of support you offer as well as to the quality of reasoning in the discourse as a whole.

E. Be especially strict about the *quality of inference* in the paper. Are the generalizations reasonable? Are the cause-

and-effect relations clearly presented and linked? Are the analogies presented clear and consistent?

F. Are there any obvious *fallacies?* Remember, the more emotionally involved you are with your subject, the more prone you are to fallacious reasoning. Start with the *language.* If there is any questionable diction, it may well be that there are problems of logic as well.

G. Do you stick to the subject at hand? At any point in the discourse, do you veer into material that, while very interesting, is not really related to the point you are trying to make?

H. Does the presentation seem *objective, fair,* and *free from self-interest?* You will often argue subjects in which your self-interest is involved. For example, all of us have a self-interest in democracy and honest government. The key issue here is one of *degree;* have you been able to show that you really have no more to gain than everybody else? Check your *language.* Signs of bias and prejudice most often reveal themselves at the level of the individual word.

Kinds of Closures

Closure ends a discourse. Suggestions for closure accompany each design throughout this book, but those suggestions will not always work. As a writer, you need to keep your eye on the rhetorical situation. What do you need to close a particular piece of writing? No two discourses are the same. Purposes vary. Content varies. Readers vary. Traditional rhetoric furnishes several strategies for closure, and we want to set them together in one spot so that you can see choices when you close a discourse. (You may invent a new way to close, but be cautious since your closure fixes your reader's last impression of you.)

THE SUMMARY

One of the best known strategies for closure, summary was called "enumeration" by the ancients. To close, simply repeat in summary form the main points from the expansion section. Summary proves most useful when you have presented a good deal of material and the reader cannot be expected to recall the information or to see segments of the discourse in relation to each other. Summary can help to bring together events of the past, especially when the assembled events make a point.

The more complex the material, the greater the value of summary. In law, a summation is still central. Complex legal matters need to be brought together. Judges and jurors need to be reminded of points of evidence developed hours, days, or weeks before. But what happens in law does not normally happen in the kinds of writing students or professionals usually do. Often in writing short essays or reports, a summary becomes unnecessary and can deaden the impact of points previously made. Who wants to hear a dry repetition of what has just been presented, especially if it is not complex? Such summary cannot only bore; it can also insult a reader. The writer seems to distrust the reader's memory. Or the reader sees the summary as padding as if the writer is attempting to lengthen the discourse, make it appear more formidable than it is, or avoid drawing conclusions about the material. Be sure that a summary will help your reader.

Here is an effective summary:

> In summary, let me state we are not on the brink of ecological disaster. Our O_2 is not disappearing. There will be no build up of poisonous CO. The waters can be made pure again by adequate sewage treatment plants. The disappearance of species is natural. A large percentage of pollution is natural pollution and would be here whether or not man was on this earth. We cannot solve our real problems unless we attack them on the basis of what we know rather than what we don't know. Let us use our knowledge and not our fears to solve the real problems of our environment.
>
> —John J. McKetta

THE APPEAL

Sometimes a writer will conclude with an appeal to something that has been implied in an argument, but not presented directly. Appeals appear only in argument. Often the appeal is emotional, but it grows directly from what has gone before.

Here is an example of closing with an appeal:

> **On the whole, Sir, I cannot help expressing a wish, that every member of the convention who may still have objections to it, would with me on this occasion doubt a little of his own infallibility, and, to make *manifest* our *unanimity*, put his name to this instrument.**
>
> **—Benjamin Franklin**

The essay by Roger M. Williams on p. 159 also ends with an appeal:

> **Because of pressures from alumni and others who exalt the role of football, Vanderbilt is still attempting to resolve this dilemma; and it is still failing. Now it is time for all the Vanderbilts and all the Alabamas to try to be Harvard whenever they can and Small-Time State on Saturday.**

THE QUESTION

Shelley concludes his "Ode to the West Wind" with the famous line, "If winter comes, can spring be far behind?" Timed correctly, questions have power. A writer chooses not to reach a clearly stated conclusion, but to leave a reader with an implication. A question assumes that a reader has much information to digest but that the information has been lined up in such a way that a single conclusion is inevitable. The writer invites the reader to participate in forming the conclusion and in seeing its implications.

Here is a closure using a question:

> **To be sure, the Russians did not invent arms or drug trafficking, any more than they invented terrorism or political assassination. But now they appear to be actively involved at both ends (M-19's military leader, Jaime Bateman, spent some time in Moscow, for example), and this involvement gives the traffickers and the terrorists a new strength. Yuri Andropov's old orga-**

nization, the K.G.B., has apparently become a major backer of drug smugglers, arms runners, and terrorists, despite the risks of discovery, despite the old reticence to dabble in such corrupt practices, and despite the current backlash against these operations. Are they really so desperate for money? Or have they gotten hooked themselves?

—Michael Ledeen, "K.G.B. Connections"

RESTATEMENT OF THE MAIN POINT

Because the development of the discourse has taken the reader's attention, writers often need to bring the reader back to the main point now that its implications have been fully developed. But such a restatement does not summarize the main points of the essay. Instead, it phrases, *in different words*, the main point. Restating can reveal dimensions not suggested in the original statement and give the writer the chance to state more precisely the purpose of the discourse.

Here is a restatement showing both the original statement and the restatement:

President Reagan, the man whom almost all union leaders regard as their implacable foe, may ultimately be a source of revitalization for organized labor in this country. (Statement)

And perhaps, through such labor-management cooperation, the unions and their counterparts in management could help create the kind of prosperity that they so firmly contend this Labor Day might come about with the end of "Reagonomics." (Restatement)

—Harry Bernstein

(See the full article on p. 156.)

JUST END

Sometimes a discourse needs no real conclusion. It ends naturally when the writer has finished developing each of his or her points. When that happens, just end.